STOKE·ON·TRENT

ESTATE PUBLICATIONS
Bridewell House,
Tenterden, Kent.
TN30 6EP
Tel: 01580 764225

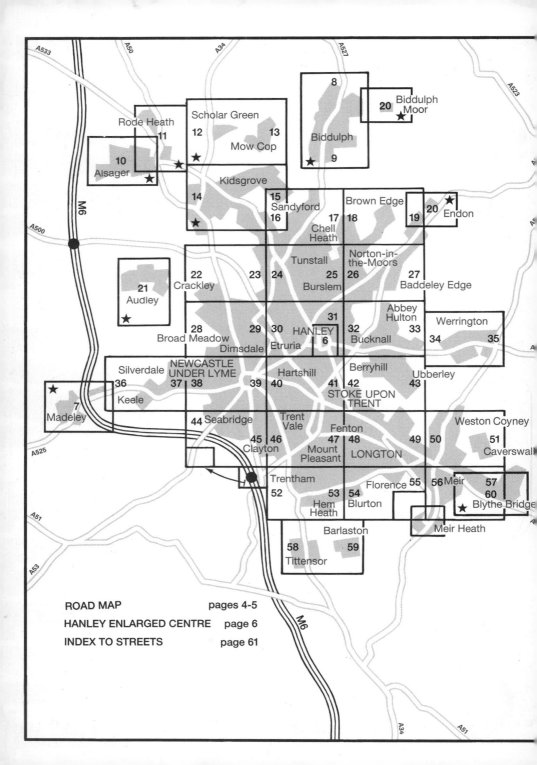

ROAD MAP   pages 4-5
HANLEY ENLARGED CENTRE   page 6
INDEX TO STREETS   page 61

ESTATE PUBLICATIONS

STOKE·ON·TRENT

NEWCASTLE·UNDER·LYME

ALSAGER · AUDLEY · BIDDULPH
BLYTHE BRIDGE · KIDSGROVE · MADELEY

Every effort has been made to verify the
accuracy of information in this book
but the publishers cannot accept
responsibility for expense or loss caused
by any error or omission. Information
that will be of assistance to the user of
the maps will be welcomed.

The representation of a road, track or
footpath on the maps in this atlas is no
evidence of the existence of a right of way.

One-way Street	→
Car Park	🅿
Place of Worship	✚
Post Office	●
Public Convenience	⊙
Pedestrianized	▨

Scale of street plans: 5 inches to 1 mile
& pages marked ★ 4 inches to 1 mile

Street plans prepared and published by ESTATE PUBLICATIONS, Bridewell House,
TENTERDEN, KENT. The Publishers acknowledge the co-operation of the
local authorities of towns represented in this atlas.

Ordnance Survey® This product includes mapping data licensed from Ordnance Survey®
with the permission of the Controller of Her Majesty's Stationery Office.

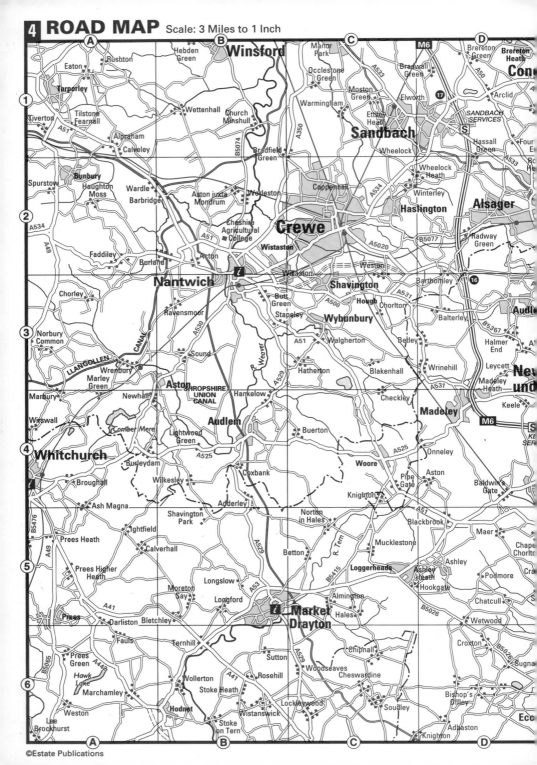

ROAD MAP

4 **ROAD MAP** Scale: 3 Miles to 1 Inch

©Estate Publications

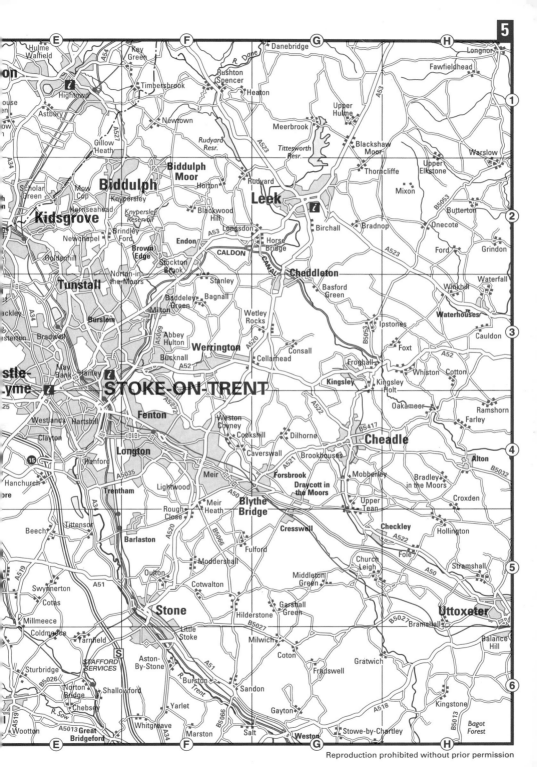

E F G H

Hulme
Walfield
Key
Green
R Dane
Danebridge
Longnor
Fawfieldhead

Hightown
Timberbrook
Rushton
Spencer
Heaton
Upper
Hulme
Astbury
Newtown
Meerbrook
Blackshaw
Moor
Warslow

Gillow
Heath
Rudyard
Resr.
Tittesworth
Resr.
Thorncliffe
Upper
Elkstone

Biddulph
Moor
Horton
Rudyard
Mixon
B5053
Butterton

Biddulph
Leek
Onecote

Scholar
Green
Mow
Cop
Knypersley
Blackwood
Hill
Birchall
Bradnop
Ford
Grindon

Kidsgrove
Hanseahead
Knypersley
Reservoir
Longsdon
A53
Horse
Bridge
CALDON
Waterfall

Newchapel
Brindley
Ford
Endon
CANAL
Cheddleton
Wakhill

Boldenhill
Brown
Edge
Stockton
Brook
Stanley
Basford
Green
Waterhouses

Tunstall
Norton-in-
the-Moors
Baddeley
Green
Bagnall
Ipstones
Cauldon

ackley
Milton
Wetley
Rocks
B5053
Foxt
A52

Burslem
Abbey
Hulton
Werrington
Consall
Froghall
Whiston
Cotton

sterton
Bradwell
Bucknall
A520
Cellarhead
Kingsley
Kingsley
Holt
Oakamoor
Ramshorn
Farley

May
Bank
Hanley
A52
STOKE-ON-TRENT
A522
Cheadle

stle-
yme
Fenton
Weston
Coyney
Dilhorne
B5417
Alton
B5032

25
Westlands
Hartshill
Cookshill
Brookhouses
Croxden

Clayton
Caverswall
A521
Mobberley
Bradley
in the Moors

15
Hanford
Longton
Meir
Forsbrook
Draycott in
the Moors
Upper
Tean

Hanchurch
ore
Trentham
Lightwood
A50
Blythe
Bridge
Cresswell
Checkley
Fole
Hollington

Beech
Tittensor
Meir
Heath
B5066
Fulford
Church
Leigh
Stramshall

Barlaston
Rough
Close
A520
Moddershall
Middleton
Green
Hilderstone

Swynnerton
Cotes
A51
Oulton
Cotwalton
Garshall
Green
Uttoxeter

Millmeece
Coldmeece
Stone
Milwich
B5027
Balance
Hill

Sturbridge
S
STAFFORD
SERVICES
Aston-
By-Stone
A51
Coton
Gratwich
Bramshall

B5026
Norton
Bridge
Shallowford
R Burston
R Trent
Sandon
Fradswell
Kingstone

Chebsey
Yarlet
Gayton
A518
B5013
Bagot
Forest

Wootton
A5013
Great
Bridgeford
Whitgreave
Marston
Salt
Weston
Stowe-by-Chartley

1 2 3 4 5 6

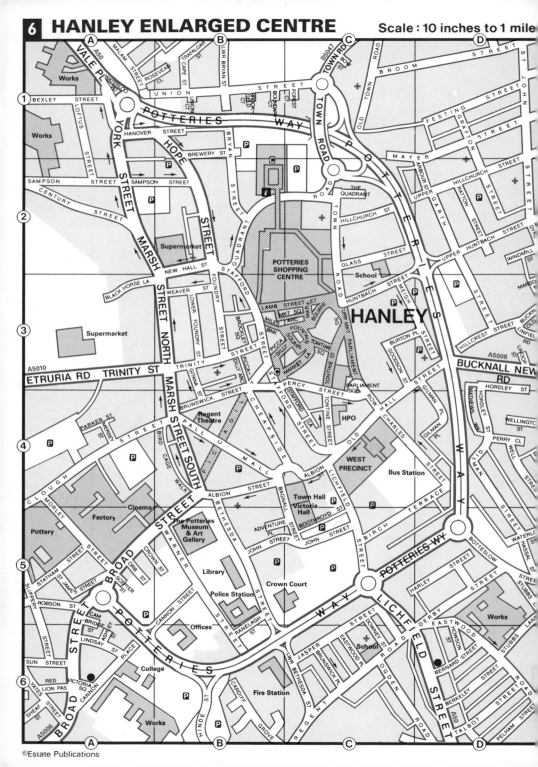

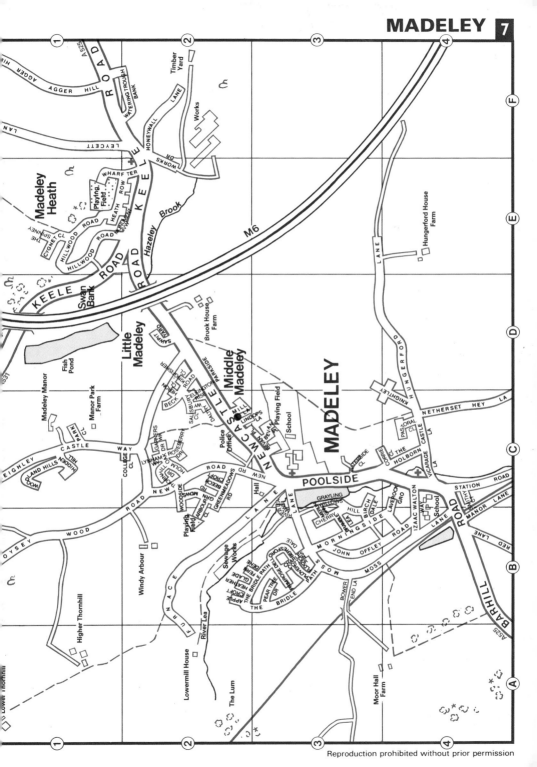

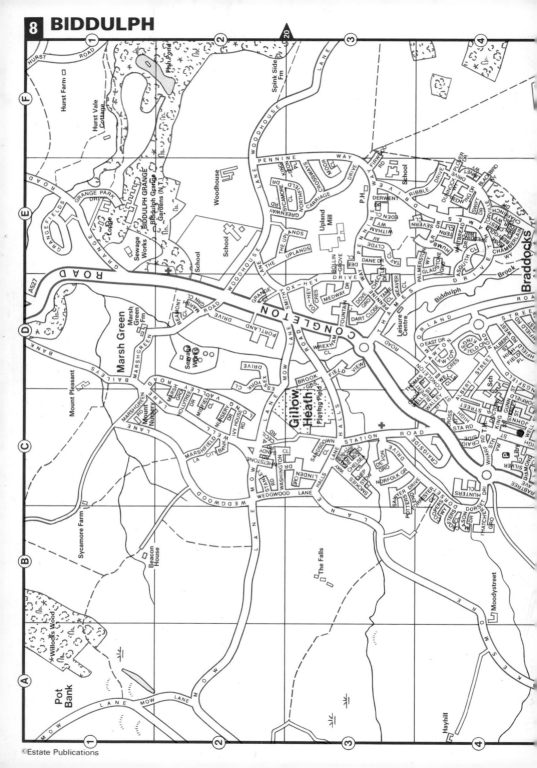

8 BIDDULPH

©Estate Publications

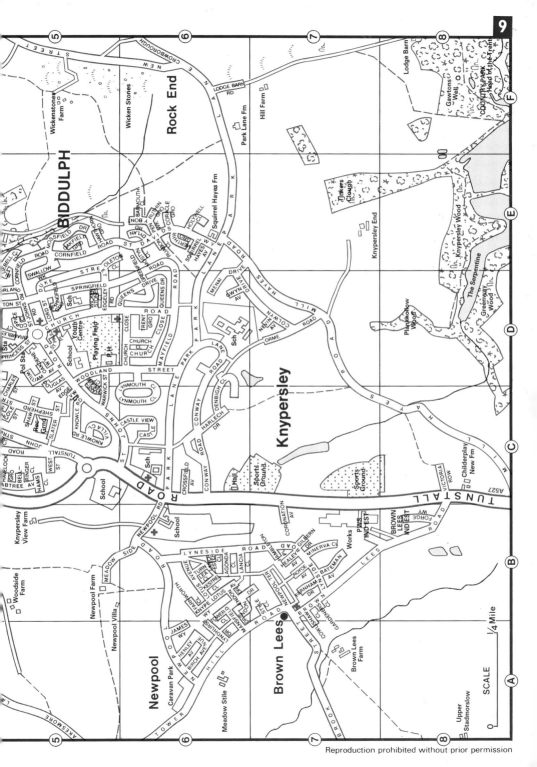

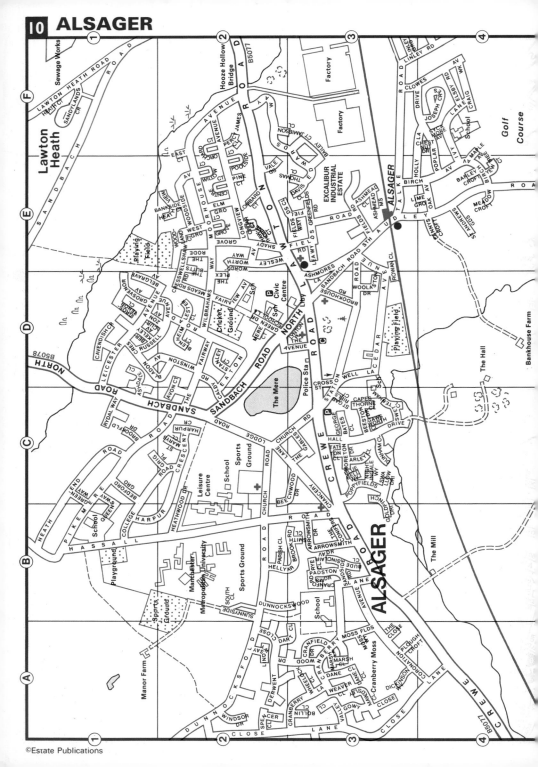

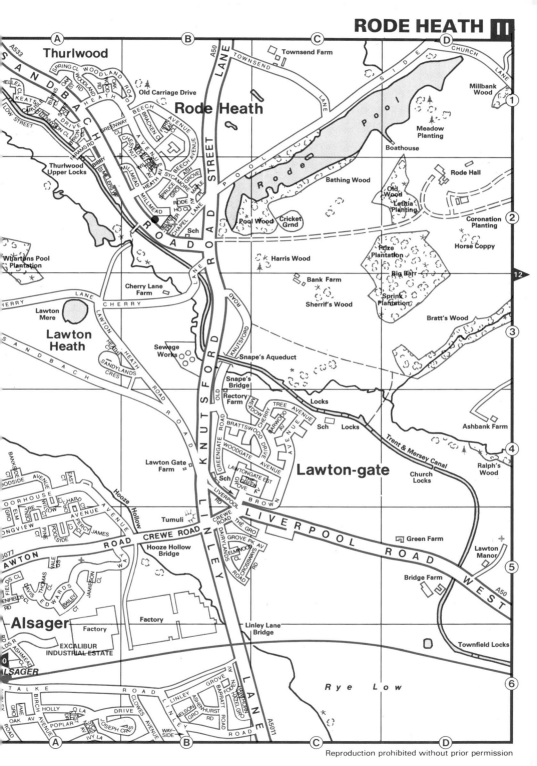

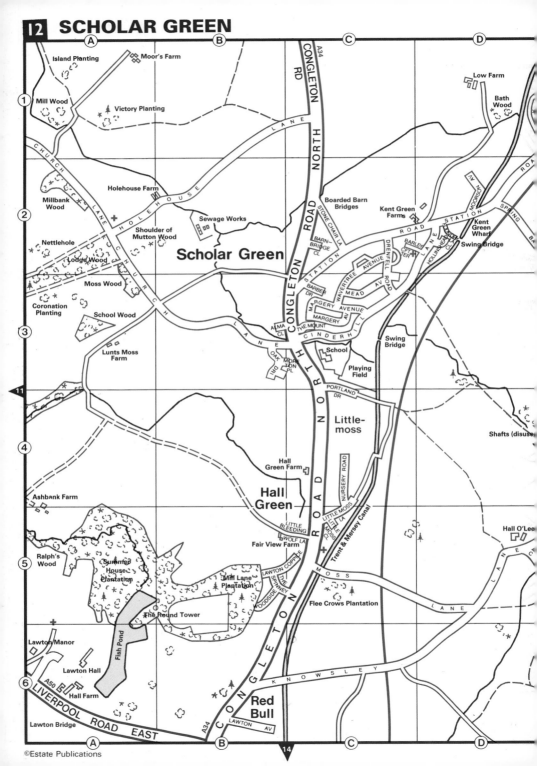

Scholar Green

Hall Green

Little-moss

Red Bull

Island Planting
Moor's Farm
Mill Wood
Victory Planting
Low Farm
Bath Wood
Holehouse Farm
Millbank Wood
Sewage Works
Boarded Barn Bridges
Kent Green Farms
Kent Green Wharf
Swing Bridge
Nettlehole
Shoulder of Mutton Wood
Lodge Wood
Moss Wood
Coronation Planting
School Wood
Swing Bridge
School
Lunts Moss Farm
Playing Field
Shafts (disused)
Hall Green Farm
Nursery Road
Ashbank Farm
Hall O'Lee
Little Bleeding
Fair View Farm
Wolf La
Ralph's Wood
Summer House Plantation
Mill Lane Plantation
Lawton Coppice
The Spinney
Woodside
Flee Crows Plantation
Trent & Mersey Canal
The Round Tower
Lawton Manor
Fish Pond
Lawton Hall
Hall Farm
Lawton Bridge
Liverpool Road East
Knowsley
Lawton Av

CONGLETON RD
CONGLETON ROAD NORTH
A34
CHURCH LANE
HOLEHOUSE LANE
STONE CHAIR LA
BARN-BRIDGE CL
STATION ROAD
DRENFELL
MOODSON AV
SPRING
WAVERTREE AVENUE
MEAD AV
MARGERY AVENUE
MARGERY
THE MOUNT
CINDERHILL
ALMA CL
OAK DRI
MORETON PL
PORTLAND DR
CONGLETON ROAD NORTH
MOSS LANE
LITTLE MOSS LA
KNOWSLEY
LANE

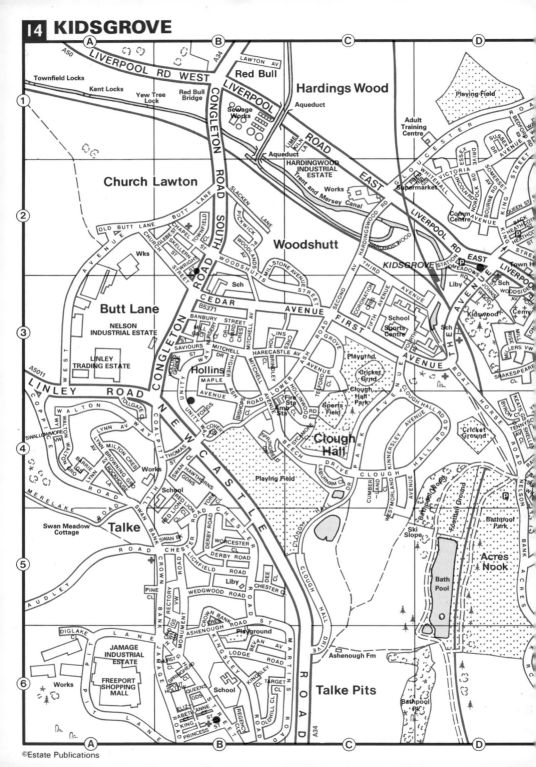

The Rookery

Natural Sciences Centre

Newchapel

KIDSGROVE

LIVERPOOL ROAD

Goldenhill Golf Course

Gill Bank

Woodstock

Latebrook

Goldenhill

Ravenscliffe

Churchill Pottery

Sports Ground

Sandyford

SCALE

0   ¼ Mile

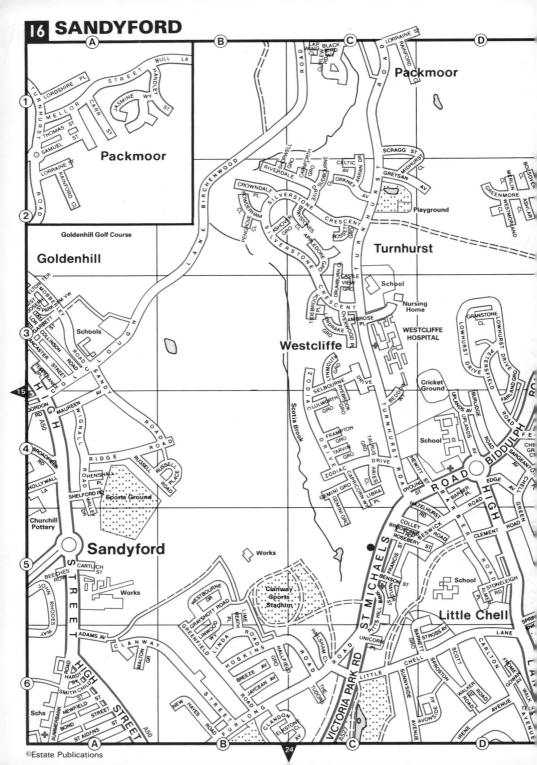

Packmoor

Goldenhill Golf Course

Goldenhill

Packmoor

Turnhurst

Westcliffe

WESTCLIFFE HOSPITAL

Nursing Home

School

Cricket Ground

School

Sports Ground

Sandyford

Churchill Pottery

Works

Works

Clanway Sports Stadium

BIDDULPH ROAD

Little Chell

School

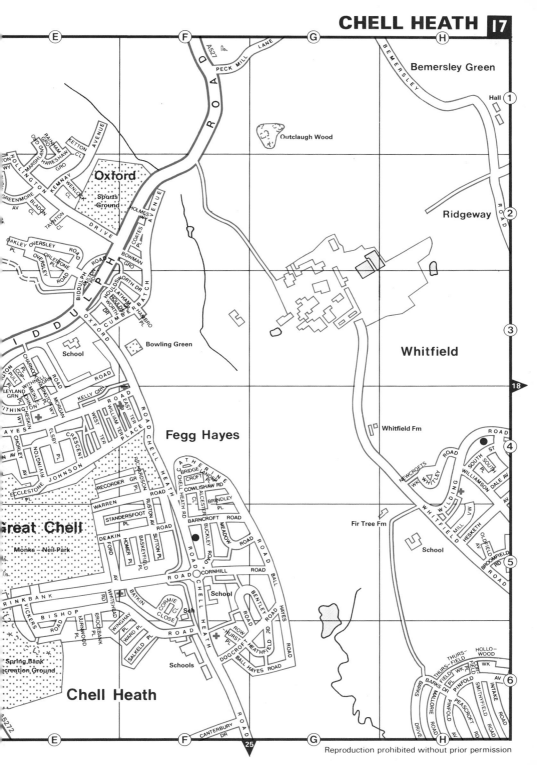

Bemersley Green

Hall

Ridgeway

Outclaugh Wood

Oxford
Sports Ground

Whitfield

Bowling Green

School

Fegg Hayes

Whitfield Fm

Great Chell

Monks – Neil Park

Fir Tree Fm

School

Spring Bank Recreation Ground

Chell Heath

School

Sch

Schools

Hollo-Wood

Ridgeway Hall

Ridgeway

Yew Tree Farm

Old Woodhouse Farm

Woodhouse Farm **Brown Edge**

School

HEATHER FARM

TEA VW

Ball Green

Head of Trent

WILDING

COWEN ST

SOUTH ST

SOUTH PL

DALE

WILLIAMSON

AVENUE

AVENUE

GREENHILL RD

MILL WK

HESKETH AV

OLDFIELD AV

NWAY

BROOMFIELD

CHET WYND

BOWER ST

ROAD

MOSS ST

BEW ST

WHITFIELD

Cornhill

KNYPERSLEY LANE

BALL GREEN

WOODHOUSE ROAD

MAPLE CL

TRENTSIDE RD

POINTON GRO

School

HARDLEY ST

ENDON ROAD

SEWORTHY

HIGH ROAD

BALL LANE

CORFIELD PL

HOLLO-WOOD WK

HOLLOWOOD

SMITHYFIELD

PINFOLD AV

INTAKE

NICHOLAS AV

FLATTS RD

ST

NICHOLAS AV

DRAKEFORD CT

HINCHO

DRAKEFORD GRO

ROAD

CHATSWORTH DR

BK TER

DUKE

VERTON CL

B5051

BLEEK

WOOD-LAND AV

LANCASTER DR

HEAKLEY

Duke Bank

Sewage Works

CLIFFORD AV

RIVERHEAD ST

FOUNDRY SQ

BALL FROBISHER ST

TRENT TER

Norton Green

LA

Heakley Hall Farm

ROAD

©Estate Publications

Ball

BROADMANS BANK

OLD LANE

NEW VAL

CHURCH ROAD

LITTLE AV

LINGFIELD

ORCHARD AV

OVERLAND DRIVE

CHURCH SYTCH

NEW C ACRES

BROWN

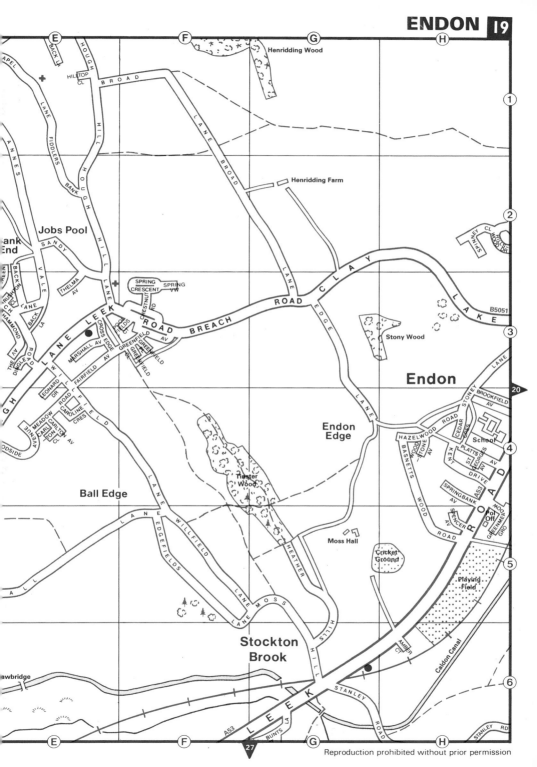

Henridding Wood

Henridding Farm

Jobs Pool

ank End

Spinney Cl

B5051

Spring Crescent
Spring Vw

BREACH ROAD
CLAY LAKE

Stony Wood

Endon

20

School

Endon Edge

Hazelwood

Ball Edge

Tinster Wood

Moss Hall

Cricket Ground

Springbank Av
A53

Playing Field

Caldon Canal

Stockton Brook

STANLEY

awbridge

A53

BUNTS LA

STANLEY RD

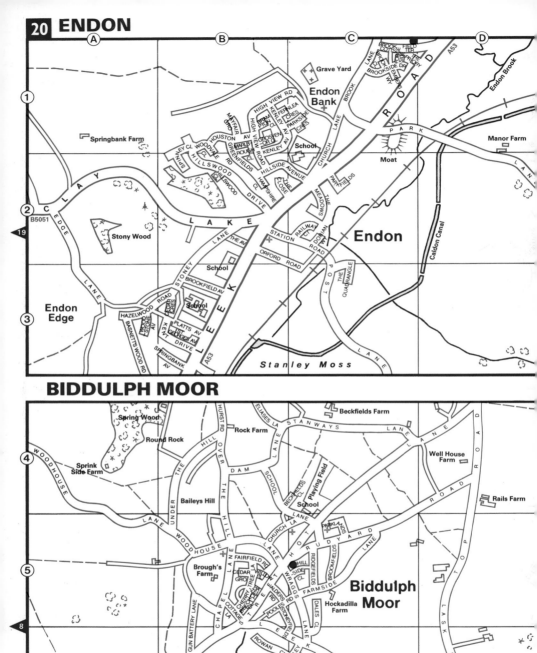

BIDDULPH MOOR

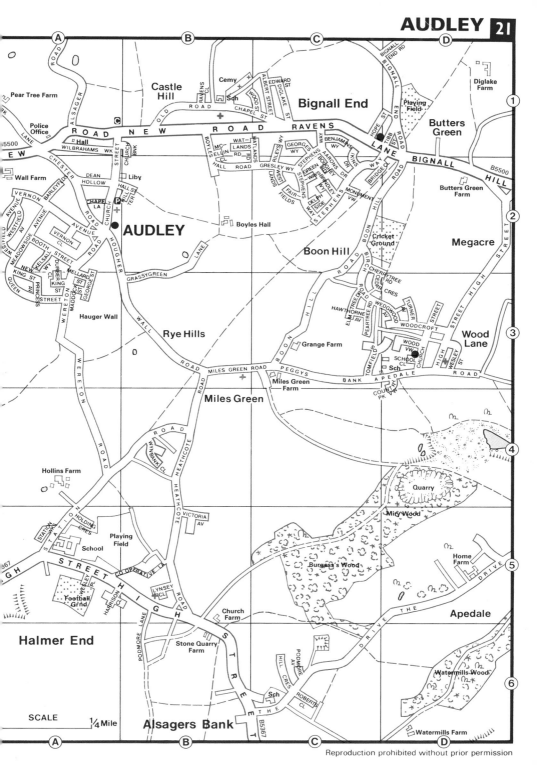

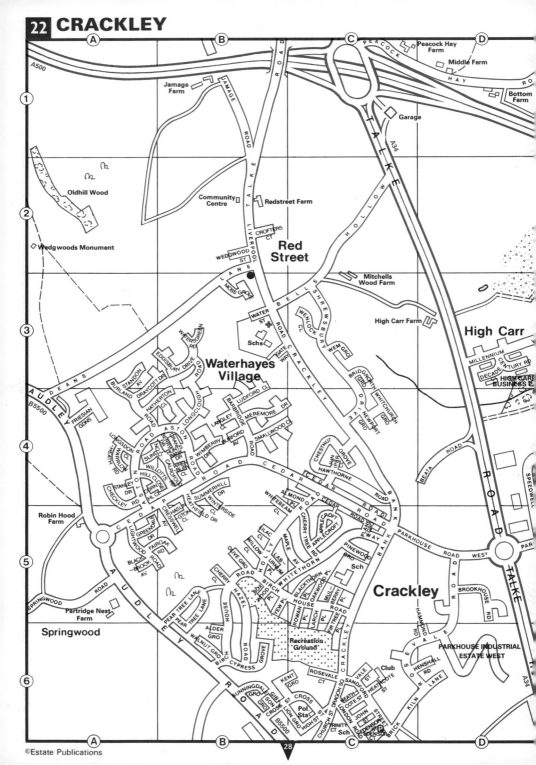

A500

A B C D

Peacock Hay Farm
Middle Farm
HAY
Bottom Farm
Jamage Farm

PEACOCK

Garage

TALKE

A34

Oldhill Wood

Community Centre
Redstreet Farm

Wedgwoods Monument

CROFTERS CT

WEDGWOOD ST

Red Street

LIVERPOOL

LANE

MOSS GROVE

Mitchells Wood Farm

HOLLOW

BELL

SHREWSBURY

WATER ST

Schs

WENLOCK CL

WEM GRO

High Carr Farm

High Carr

GATE

CRACKLEY

WAY

Waterhayes Village

WATERS GREEN RD

EDDISBURY DRIVE

DRAYCOTT DR

HATHERTON CL

LONGCLOUGH

LANGLEY

BARBRIDGE

LUDFORD CL

MEREMORE DR

SMALLWOOD CT

BRIDGNORTH GRO

WHITCHURCH GRO

NEWPORT GRO

DRIVE

MILLENNIUM
CENTURY RD
DECADE
HIGH CARR BUSINESS

STANDON AV

BURLAND

FRIESIAN GDNS

WARRILOW HEATH RD

LONGSDON

STANLEY DR

CHECKLEY RD

HILL CL

WILLOTTS

ASTON RD

ROAD

ROAD

WIMBERRY

RUFFORD AV

ROAD

CHESTNUT GROVE

HAWTHORNE

CEDAR

DEANS

AUDLEY
B5500

Robin Hood Farm

SUMMERHILL DR
WINTERSIDE
HEATHFIELD DR

GREEN
FAIROAK RD

CRESSWELL

WHITEBEAM

ALMOND
CL

CHERRY TREE RD

APPLECROFT

APPLECROFT

CEDAR

ROAD

ROAD WEST

PARKHOUSE ROAD WEST

BEATA

ROAD

TALKE

SPEEDWELL

LIGHTWOOD DR
BLACKBROOK AV

CHERRY TREE CL

OLIVE GRO
WILLOW

ILAC
LILAC
LABURNUM

MAPLE AV

BIRCH

WHITETHORN

PINEWOOD

PRO Sch

Springwood

Partridge Nest Farm

SPRINGWOOD

PEAR TREE LANE

WALNUT GRO

BIRCH

CYPRESS

HAZEL

HOUSE

CEDAR

BOXWOOD PL
YEW PL

ROWAN PL
LARCH PL

HOLLY
MULBERRY PL

BLACKTHORN
OAKWOOD PL

PL

Crackley

BROOKHOUSE RD

HAMMOND

ROSEVALE

PARKHOUSE INDUSTRIAL ESTATE WEST

Recreation Ground

ALDER GRO

KENT GRO

ROSEVALE CT

VALE ST

Club

HENSHALL RD

KILN

BUNNINGDALE GRO
GIBSON GRO

COTE ST
CROSS ST

CROSS

LION GRO

HIGH ST

SANDFORD

COTE ST

HEATHCOTE ST

CHURCH ST
DRAGON SQ
LONDON
TRINITY CT Sch

JOHN ST
SPENSER

BRICK

Pol Sta

B5500

Springwood

AUDLEY

ROAD

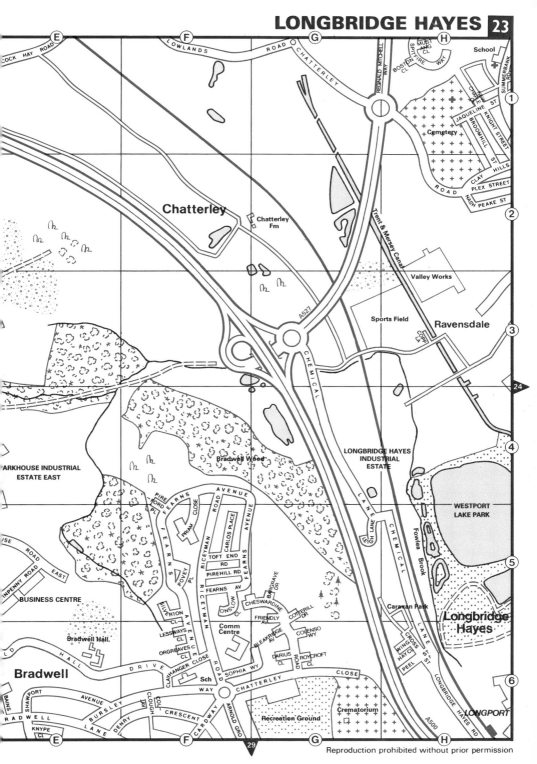

Map labels:

E F G H

LOWLANDS ROAD
COCK HAY ROAD
CHATTERLEY
REGINALD MITCHELL WAY
BOSTON CL
SPITFIRE WAY
MUST ANG CL
School
SUMMERBANK RD
CHAPLE ST
KNIGHT STREET
BROOMHILL ST
JAQUELINE ST
Cemetery
CLAY HILLS
PLEX STREET
NASH ROAD
PEAKE ST

Chatterley
Chatterley Fm

Trent & Mersey Canal
Valley Works
Ravensdale
Sports Field
COPPI CLA

A527

24

CHEMICAL

ARKHOUSE INDUSTRIAL ESTATE EAST
Bradwell Wood
LONGBRIDGE HAYES INDUSTRIAL ESTATE

WESTPORT LAKE PARK

Fowlea Brook

PIRE FORD PL
FEARNS
AVENUE
PRIM CLOSE
RICEYMAN ROAD
CARLOS PLACE
POVEY PL
TOFT END RD
PIREHILL RD
FEARNS AV
FEARNS AVENUE
ONSLOW
SILVERTON CL
CHESWARDINE
BARGRAVE DR
COTTERILL DR
FRIENDLY AV
LESSWAYS CL
ORGREAVES CL
Comm Centre
CLAYHANGER CLOSE
BLEARIDGE AV
COVENSO WY
DARIUS CL
ROYCROFT CL
SOPHIA WY
Sch
CAROVAN PARK
Longbridge Hayes
WINGROSS
HAY CL
PEEL
CROSS ST
LANE

BUSINESS CENTRE
Bradwell Hall
Bradwell
HALL DRIVE
SHAWPORT AVENUE
BAINS
BURSLEY LANE
RADWELL
KNYPE CL
COL DENBY
CRESCENT
CLOUGH
CARDWAY
ARNOLD GRO
CHATTERLEY WAY
Recreation Ground
Crematorium
Caravan Park
LONGBRIDGE HAYES RD
LONGPORT
A500

1
2
3
4
5
6

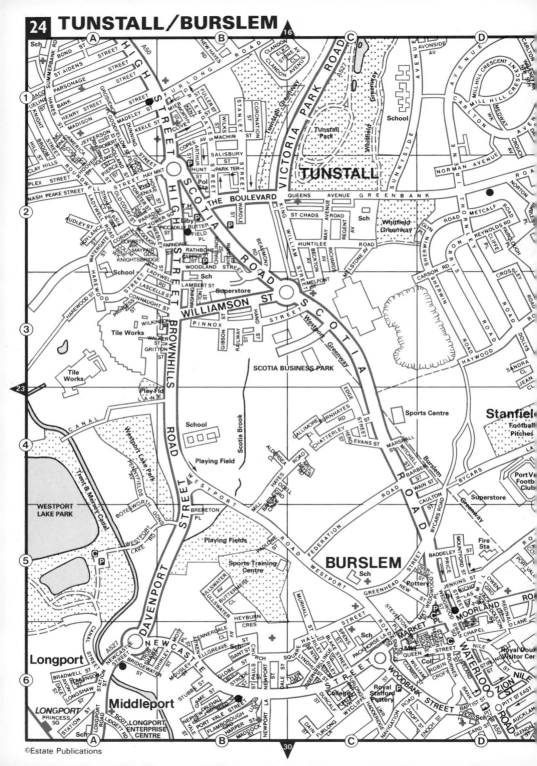

©Estate Publications

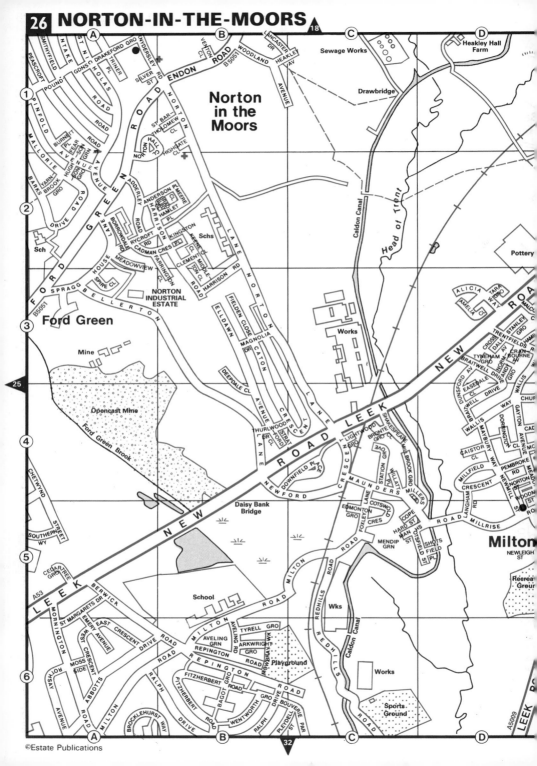

Norton in the Moors

Sewage Works

Heakley Hall Farm

Drawbridge

Caldon Canal

Head of Trent

Pottery

Works

NORTON INDUSTRIAL ESTATE

Ford Green

Mine

Opencast Mine

Ford Green Brook

Daisy Bank Bridge

Downfield Pl

Newford

NEW LEEK ROAD

School

Playground

Wks

Works

Caldon Canal

Sports Ground

Milton

Recrea Groun

NEWLEIGH ST

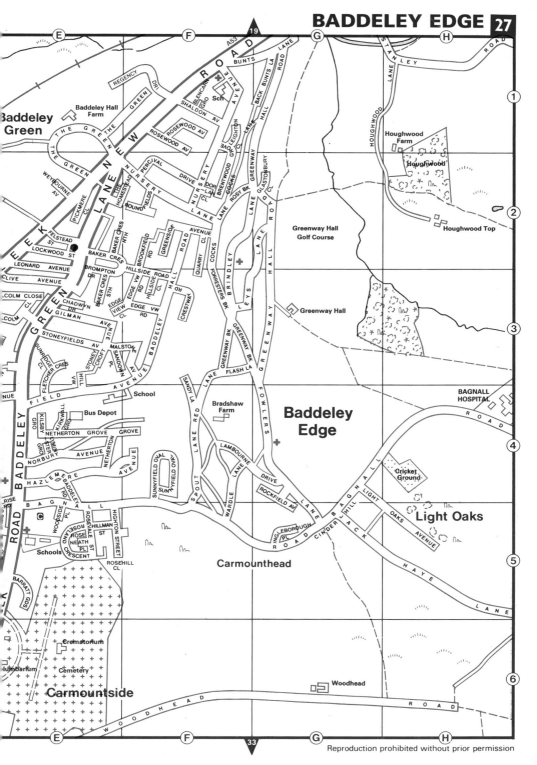

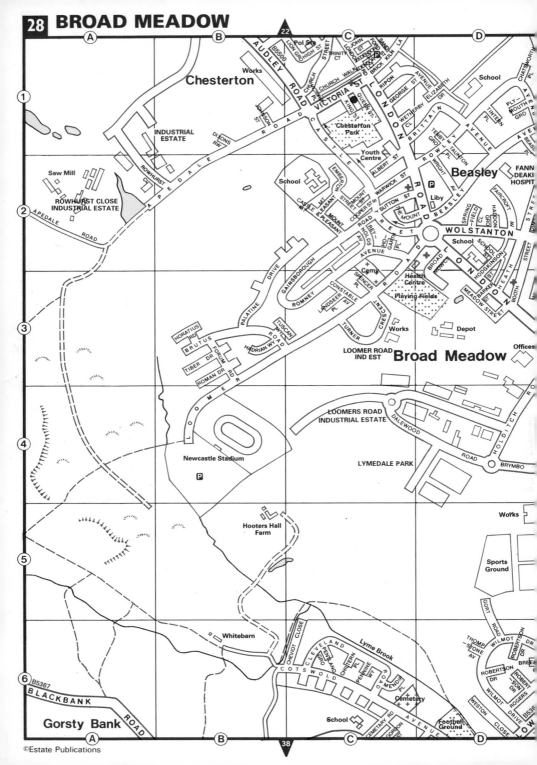

Chesterton

Beasley

FANN
DEAKI
HOSPIT

WOLSTANTON

Broad Meadow

LOOMER ROAD
IND EST

LOOMERS ROAD
INDUSTRIAL ESTATE

LYMEDALE PARK

BRYMBO

Newcastle Stadium

Hooters Hall
Farm

Sports
Ground

Works

INDUSTRIAL
ESTATE

ROWHURST CLOSE
INDUSTRIAL ESTATE

Saw Mill

APEDALE ROAD

Works

Depot

Offices

Whitebarn

Lyme Brook

BLACKBANK ROAD

Gorsty Bank

School

Cemetery

Football
Ground

Chesterton
Park

Youth
Centre

School

Health
Centre

Playing Fields

AUDLEY ROAD

VICTORIA ST

LONDON ROAD

©Estate Publications

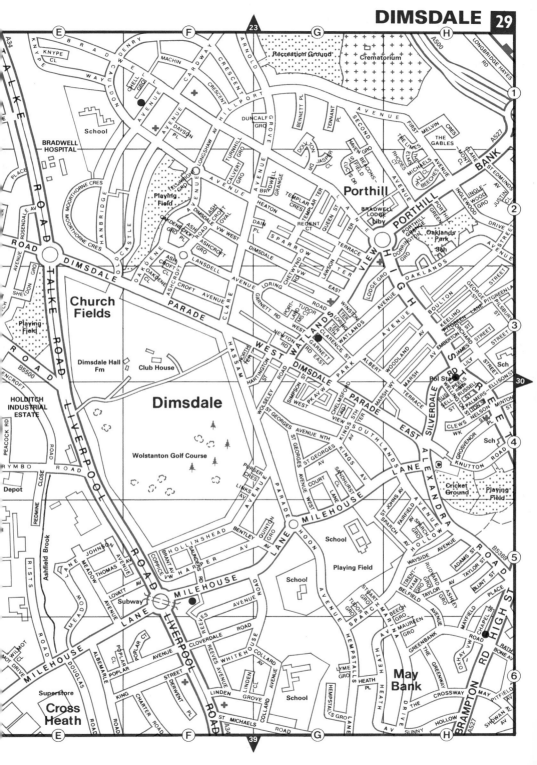

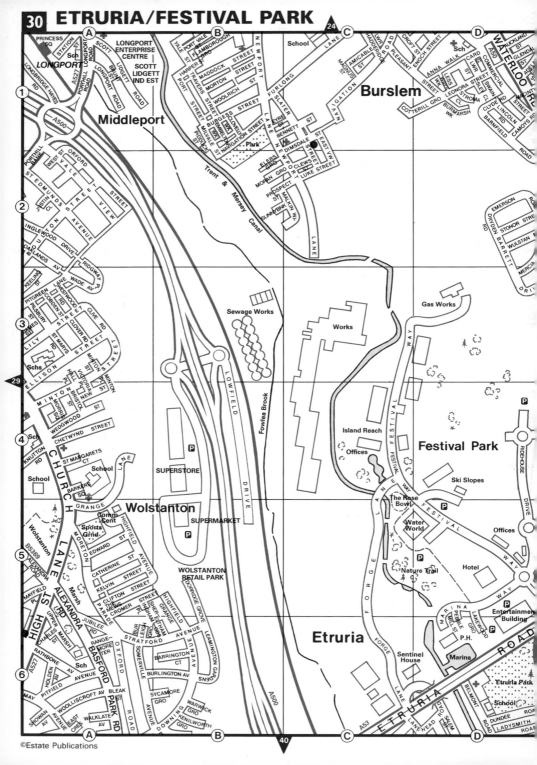

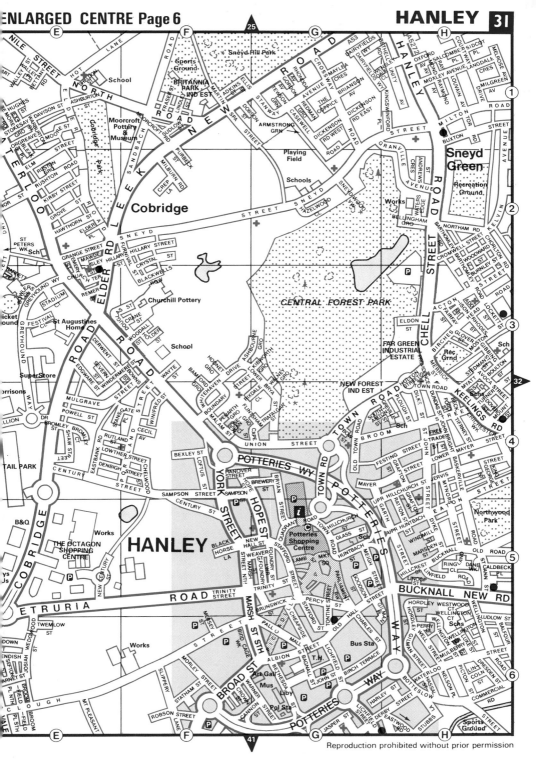

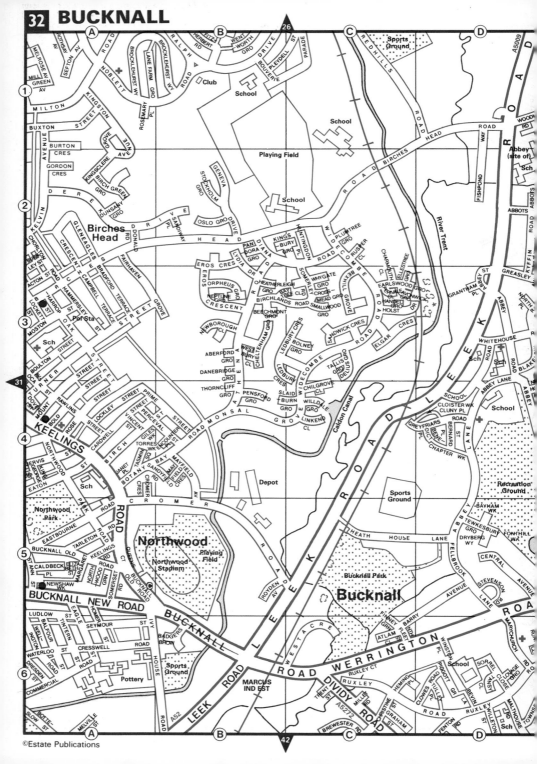

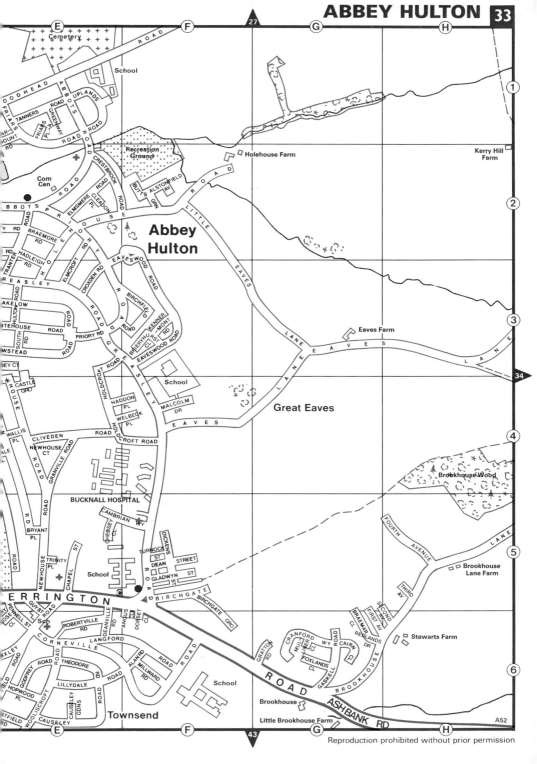

Abbey Hulton

Great Eaves

Bucknall Hospital

Townsend

Cemetery

School

Recreation Ground

Holehouse Farm

Kerry Hill Farm

Eaves Farm

Brookhouse Wood

Brookhouse Lane Farm

Stewarts Farm

Brookhouse

Little Brookhouse Farm

Com Cen

27

43

34

A52

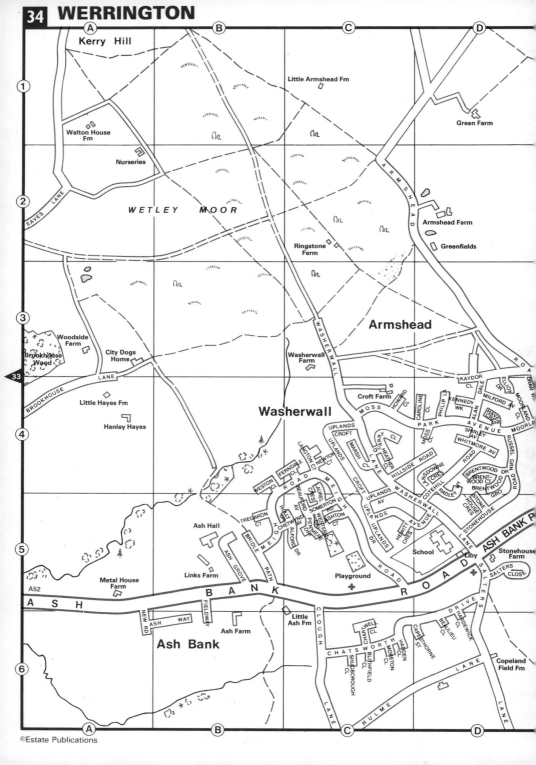

Kerry Hill

Little Armshead Fm

Green Farm

Walton House Fm

Nurseries

A R M S H E A D

Armshead Farm

Greenfields

W E T L E Y   M O O R

Ringstone Farm

Armshead

Woodside Farm

Brookhouse Wood

City Dogs Home

Washerwall Farm

W A S H E R W A L L

KAYDOR CL

ELLIOT DR

MILFORD AV

MOORLAND

DALE

HAYE CLOSE

MOORL

BROOKHOUSE LANE

Little Hayes Fm

Hanley Hayes

Croft Farm

Washerwall

UPLANDS CROFT

UPLANDS

NEWTON CT

MARSH LANE

MOSS PARK

HOWARD CL

CAROLINE CL

PHILIP LA

KENNEDY WK

ALAN

RUSSEL GRN

A V E N U E

SHIRLEY AV

WHITMORE AV

BRENTWOOD DR

BRENT-WOOD CT

BRENTWOOD GRO

ROAD

Ash Hall

FERNDALE CL

LANGTON CT

WESTON CL

BEAUFORD CT

HILLSIDE ROAD

QUAYLE AV

HEATHER CL

MOSS CL

LANSDOWNE CRES

COTEHILL

RADLEY

CROFT AV

STONE HOUSE CRES

STONEHOUSE

Links Farm

Metal House Farm

TREGARON CT

BRIDLE PATH

MEIGH ROAD

RIDLEY

CHETWIND

ALFORD DR

LAUREL CT

SOMERTON RD

ASHTON

WEBBERLEY

PENNINE DR

UPLANDS AV

UPLANDS

WASHERWALL

UPLANDS ROAD

HEWITT AV

AVENUE

HADEN CRES

School

Liby

Stonehouse Farm

Playground

SALTERS CLOSE

A52

A S H   B A N K   R O A D

NEW RD

ASH WAY

FIELDWAY

Ash Farm

Little Ash Fm

Ash Bank

CLOUGH LANE

CHATWEL

SHUGBOROUGH CL

CHATSWORTH

BLITHFIELD CL

MORETON CL

HADEN

CAPESTHORNE

BEAULIEU CL

HADDWICK

DRIVERS LANE

ST

Copeland Field Fm

HULME LANE

LANE

©Estate Publications

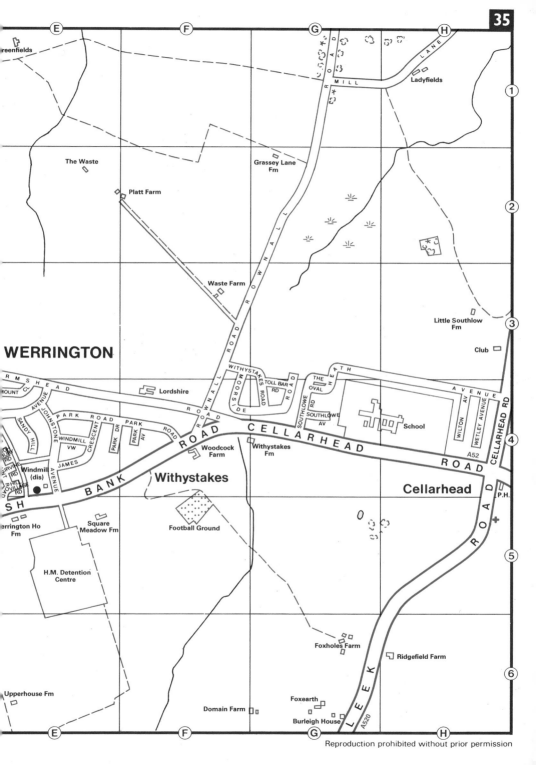

E F G H

1

Greenfields

Ladyfields

MILL ROAD
LANE

The Waste

Grassey Lane
Fm

2

Platt Farm

Waste Farm

ROWNALL ROAD

3

Little Southlow
Fm

Club

WERRINGTON

Lordshire

WITHYSTAKES
MOORSIDE
ROAD

TOLL BAR
RD

THE OVAL

SOUTHLOWE RD
SOUTHLOWE AV

HEATH

AVENUE

WILTON AV
WETLEY AVENUE

CELLARHEAD RD

4

ROWNALL ROAD

ARMSHEAD
MOUNT CT.

AVENUE
JOHNSTONE

PARK ROAD
CRESCENT
PARK DR
PARK AV

PARK ROAD

SANDY HILL
WINDMILL VW
JAMES

ROAD

CELLARHEAD

School

A52

ROAD

Woodcock
Farm

Withystakes
Fm

Windmill
(dis)

BANK

Withystakes

Cellarhead

P.H.

5

Werrington Ho
Fm

Square
Meadow Fm

Football Ground

ROAD

LEEK

H.M. Detention
Centre

Foxholes
Farm

Ridgefield Farm

6

Upperhouse Fm

Foxearth

A520

Domain Farm

Burleigh House

E F G H

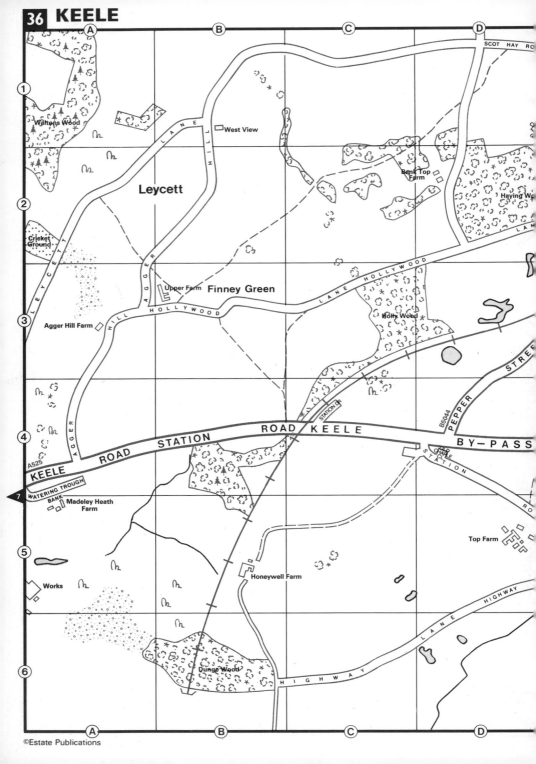

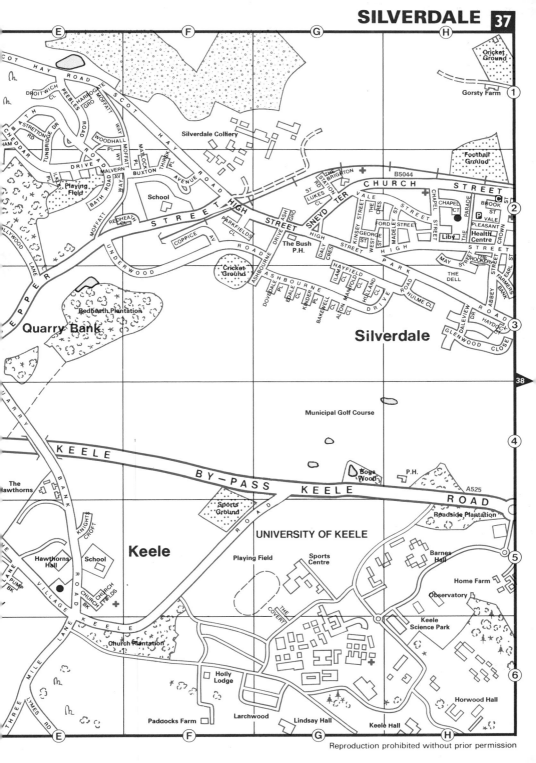

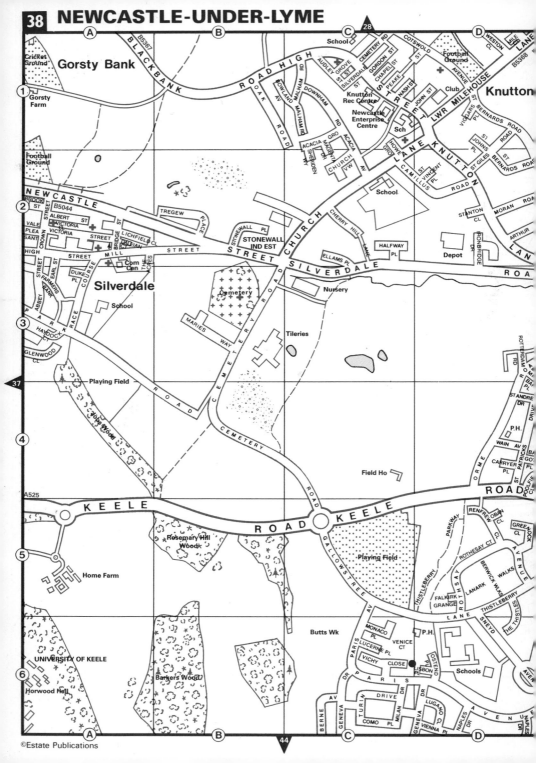

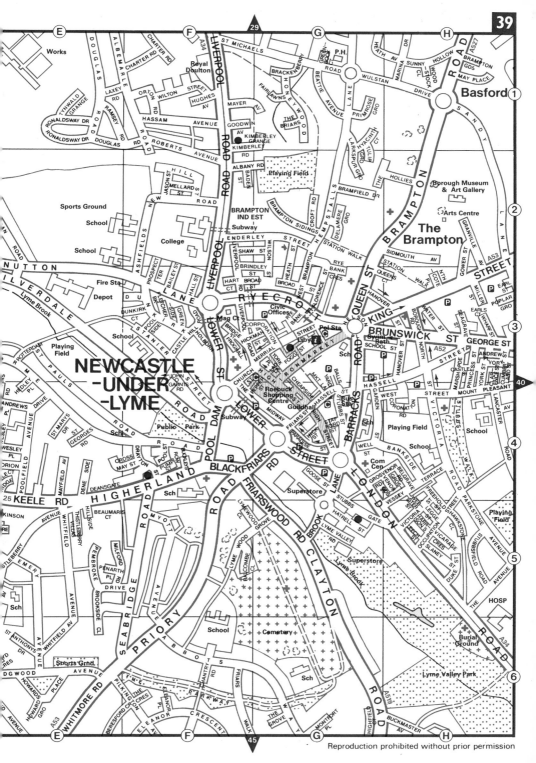

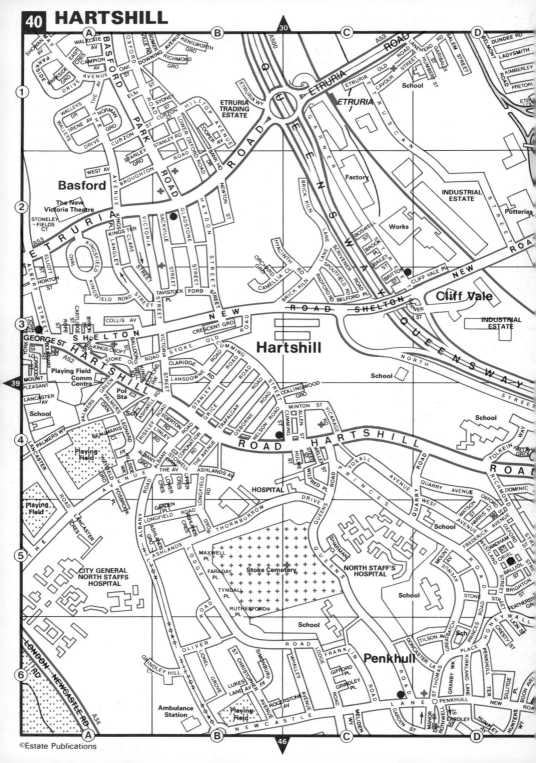

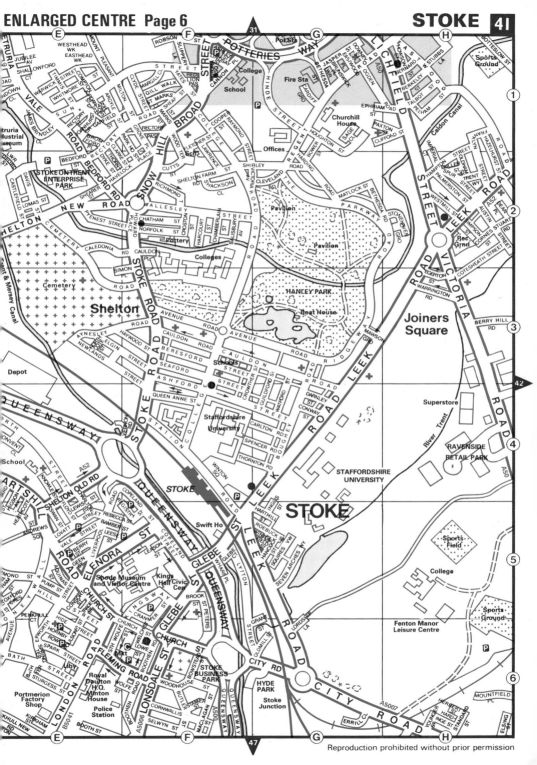

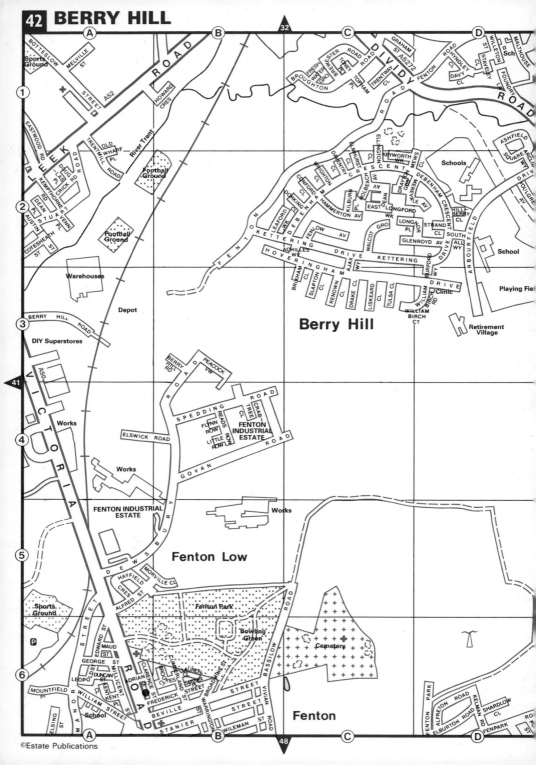

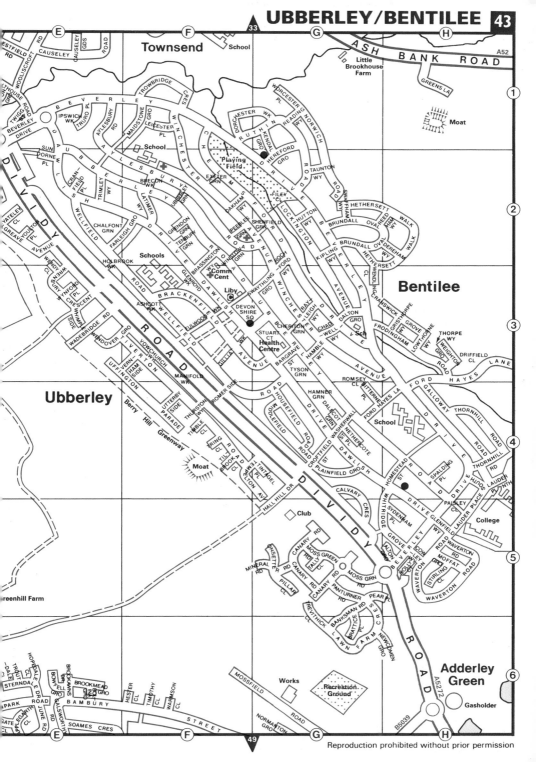

UBBERLEY/BENTILEE 43

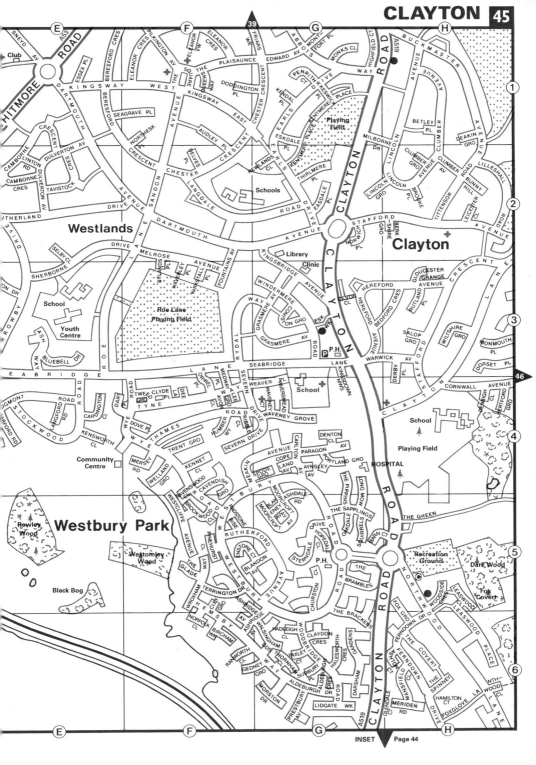

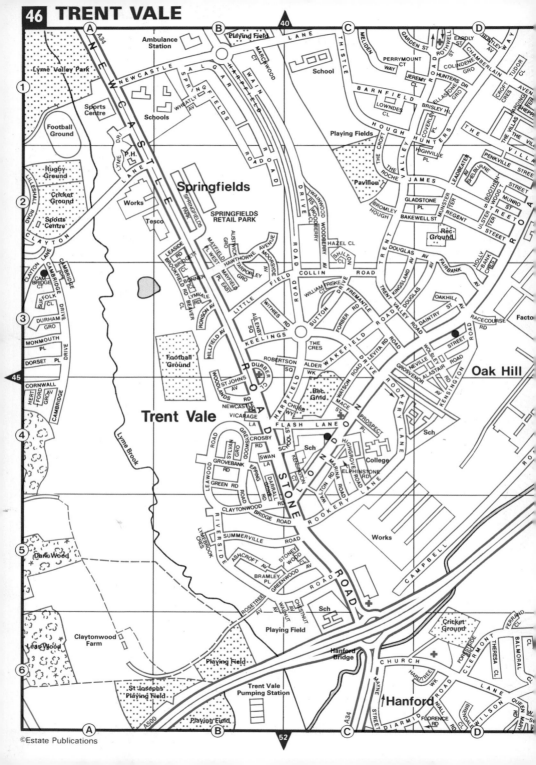

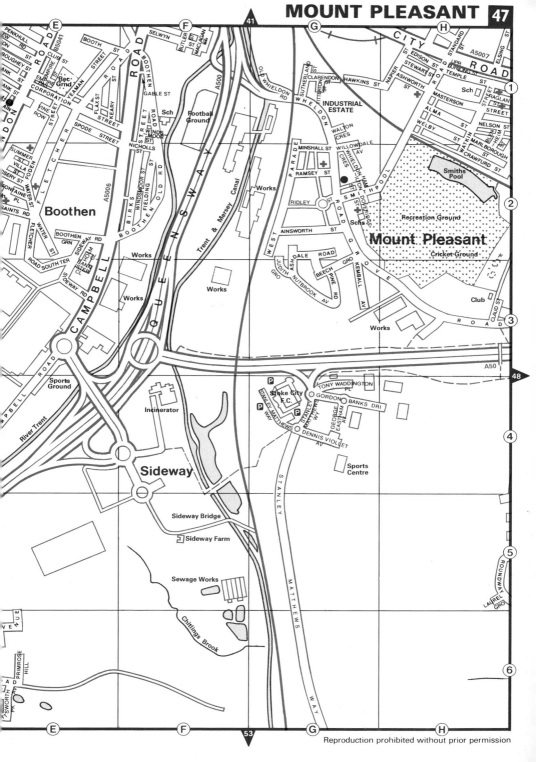

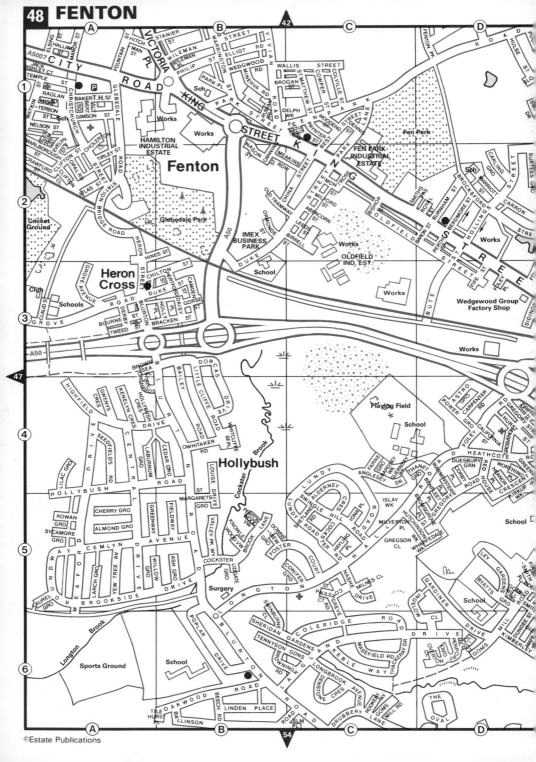

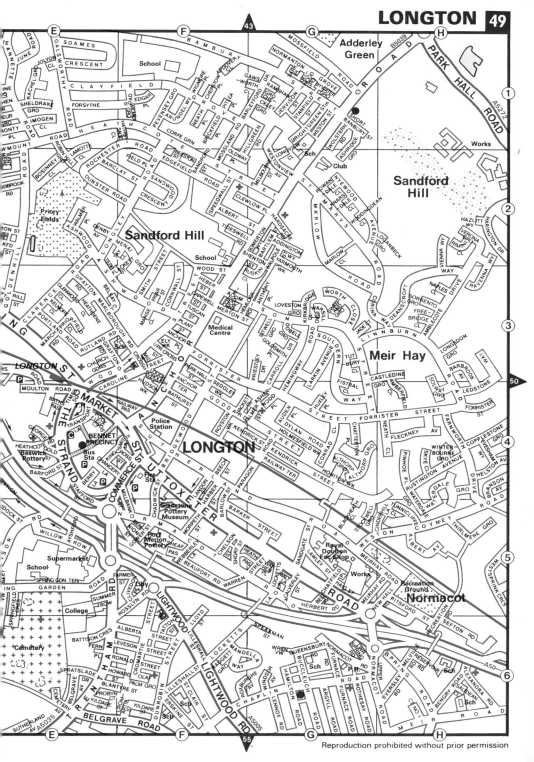

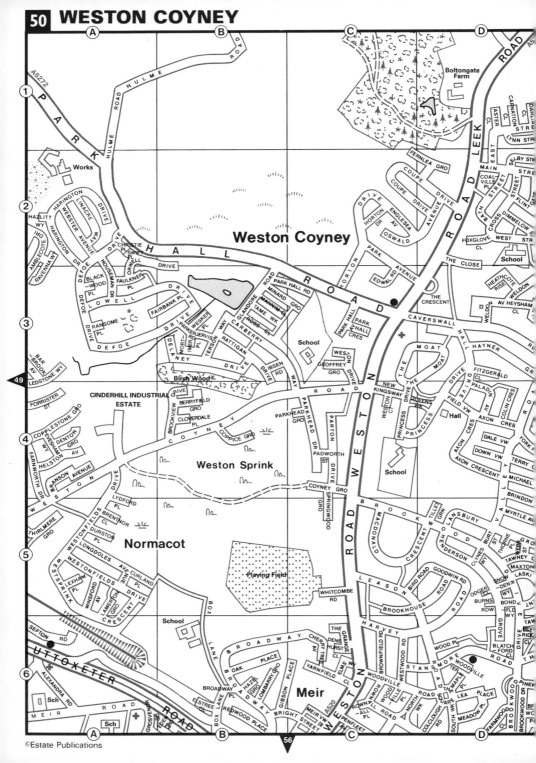

Boltongate Farm

Works

Weston Coyney

School

Birch Wood

CINDERHILL INDUSTRIAL ESTATE

Weston Sprink

Normacot

School

Meir

Playing Field

Sch

Sch

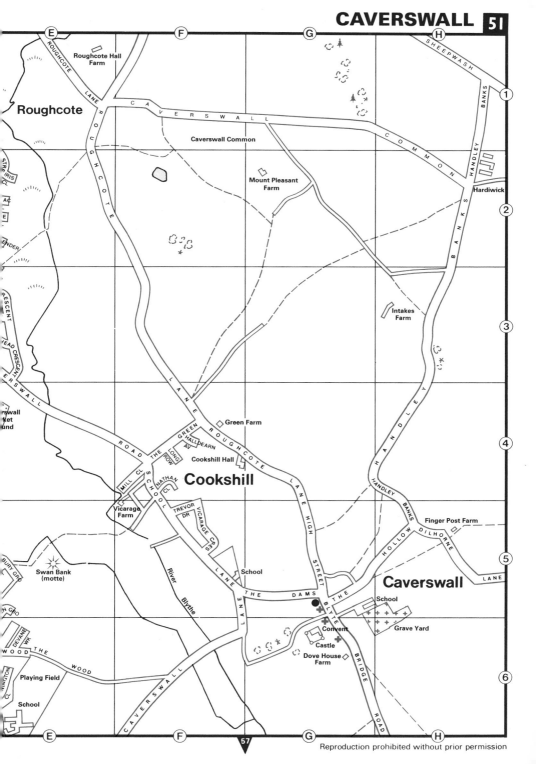

Roughcote

Roughcote Hall Farm

E

F

G

H

SHEEPWASH

ROUGHCOTE LANE

CAVERSWALL

Caverswall Common

1

BANKS

HANDLEY

Mount Pleasant Farm

Hardiwick

2

COMMON

BANKS

Intakes Farm

3

ROUGHCOTE LANE

Green Farm

HALLDEARN

GREEN

LONG ROW

Cookshill Hall

Cookshill

HANDLEY

4

MILL CL

THE

SCHOOL

NATHAN CL

TREVOR DR

VICARAGE CRES

LANE

HIGH

HANDLEY BANKS

HOLLOW

DILHORNE

Finger Post Farm

Vicarage Farm

ROAD

CRESCENT

STR IRIS CL

AC

E

ENDER

swall ket und

ERSWALL

5

School

STREET

THE DAMS

LANE

Caverswall

LANE

School

BURY GRO

Swan Bank (motte)

River Blythe

THE

BLYTHE

Convent

Castle

Grave Yard

N GRO

DEVANE WK

THE WOOD

WOOD

Dove House Farm

BRIDGE

6

Playing Field

School

CAVERSWALL

ROAD

E

F

G

H

A   B   46   C   D

1   page 44   INSET

Trent Vale
Pumping Station

Playing Field

NORTHWOOD

A500

FERNDOWN DR STH

The Limes

2   EVA GRO   MORETON AV

B5038

WHITMORE   LANE

Tumulus

Turbine
Farm

River Trent

Hargreaves Wood

FAIRWAY

Police Office

3   Hargreaves Pool

THE PARKWAY   THE GREENWAY

THE FIELDWAY   THE PARKWAY

Trentham Park
Golf Course

Baileys Pool

4   Park Brook

Trentham
Cl

HOLLYBANK DRIVE

Craft
Centre

Trentham Raceway

5   Trentham Park

Caravan Park

Playground

Italian
Gardens

Trentham Gardens
& Pleasure Grounds

Boat House

6   Kingwood Bank

STONE ROAD

A34

MAYNE ST   DIARMID RD

NEW INN LANE

LEVESON   FLORENCE ROAD

DANE HILL GRO   DANE HILL PL   DANE HILL

BRIARBANK CL   NORTHGATE CL

ANSON STREET   WILSON ROAD

KINGS ROAD   RICHMOND RD   BARNWELL GRO

WESTMINSTER CL   GEORGES CRES   EDERE RD   CARRICK   RENFREW

Recreation
Ground

AMPHILL PL   GARFIELD   GARFIELD CRES

GROVE   P.H.   BRANDON GRO

ASHENDENE PL   APLEY PL

BANKHOUSE ROAD

IVY GROVE   JUBILEE RD

School

BOMA   MARGARET AV   HIGHFIELDS RISE

ROBINSON RD

TURNBERRY DR   DEANSBERRY PL

School

PARKWOOD AV   CHURCH ROAD   PERTHY GRO

ALLERTON   CHURCHILL   CHURCHILL AVENUE

Liby   TRENTLEY DR

MALVERN PL   CRANBROOK   BAINBRIDGE DR   DELAMERE GRO

WESTERHAM CL   WERBURGH

TRENTHAM GDNS   CONISTON   WENGER   ESCONE PL   WERBURGH CRESCENT   DRIVE

SWANTON PL   Longton Brook

PARK DRIVE

STONE ROAD

LONGTON

Old Dock Rd

P   P   P   P

STONE ROAD   A34

©Estate Publications

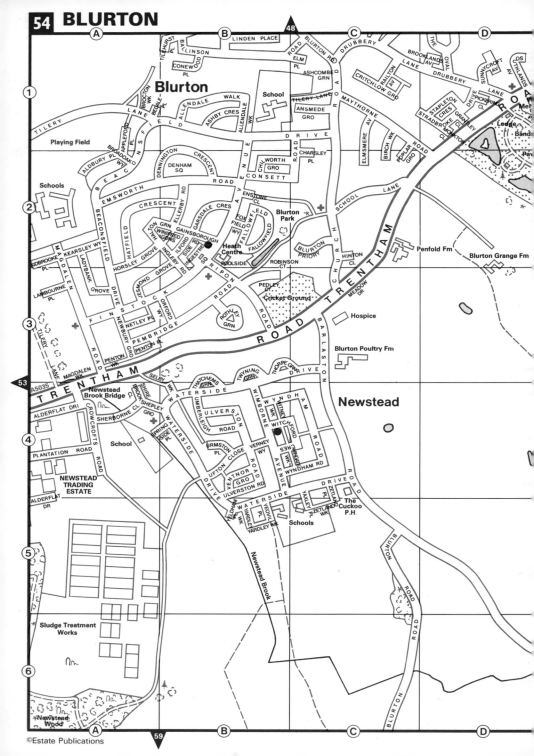

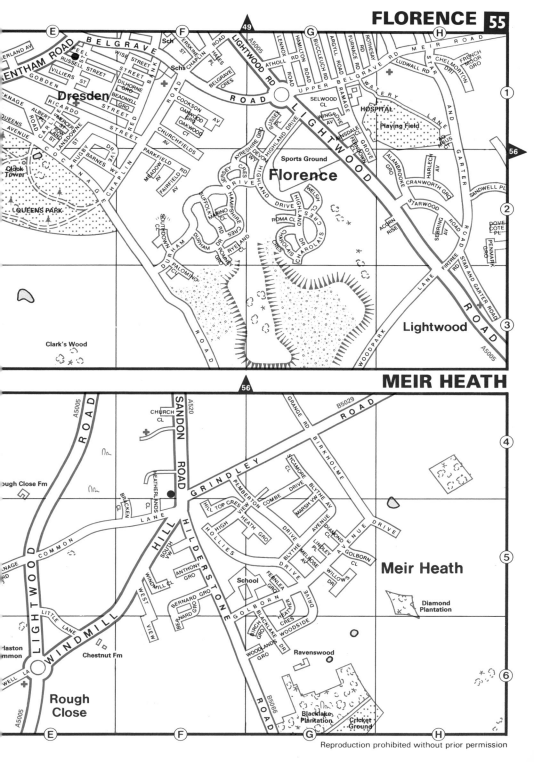

FLORENCE 55

MEIR HEATH

Dresden

Florence

Lightwood

Meir Heath

Rough Close

Queens Park

Clark's Wood

Hospital

Playing Field

Sports Ground

Clock Tower

Church Cl

Rough Close Fm

Chestnut Fm

Ravenswood

Diamond Plantation

Blacklake Plantation

Cricket Ground

School

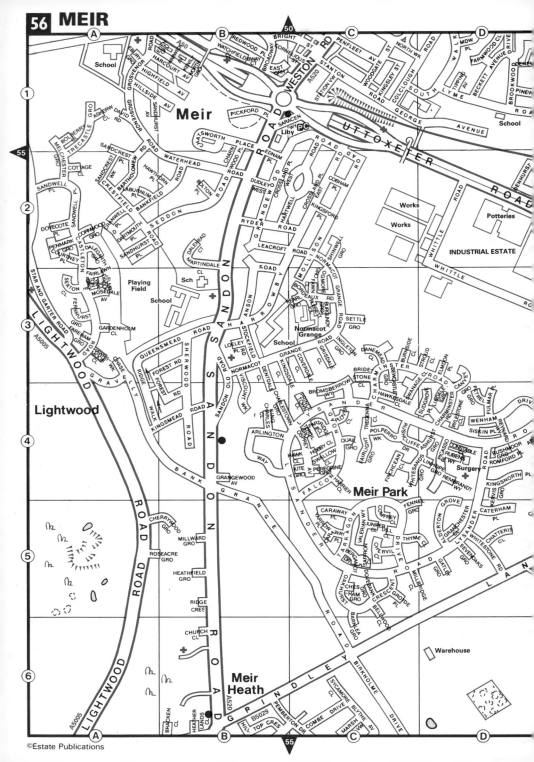

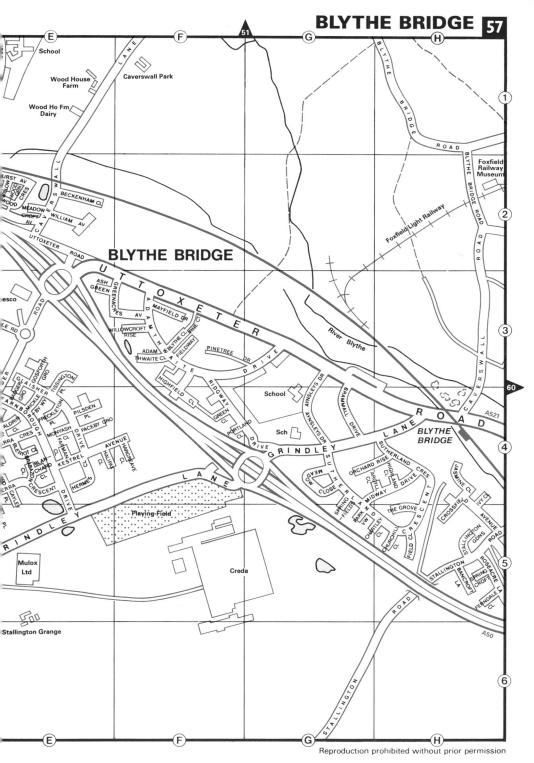

BLYTHE BRIDGE

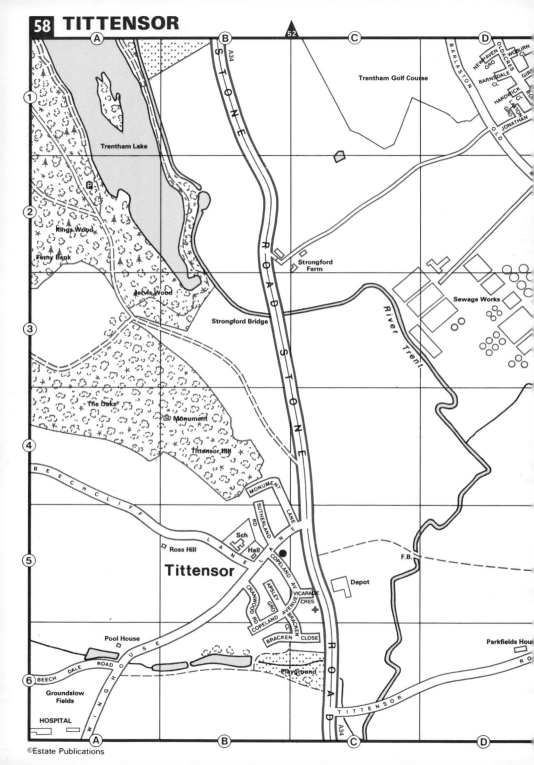

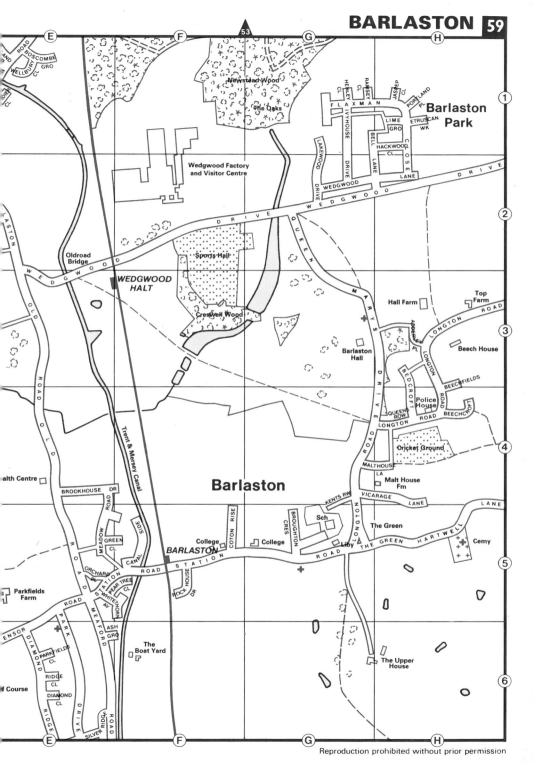

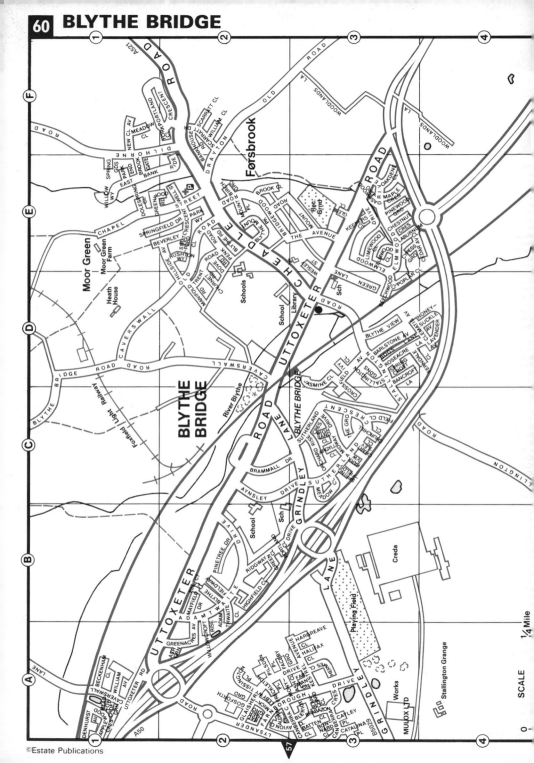

Forsbrook

Moor Green

BLYTHE BRIDGE

Creda

Stallington Grange

MULOX LTD

SCALE

¼ Mile

The Index includes some names for which there is insufficient space on the maps. These names are preceded by an * and are followed by the nearest adjoining thoroughfare

Ravens La. ST7	21 C1
Rileys Way. ST7	21 C1
Roberts Clo. ST7	21 C6
School Clo. ST7	21 D3
Station Rd. ST7	21 A5
Station Walks. ST7	21 A5
Stephens Way. ST7	21 C2
The Drive. ST7	21 C6
Tibb St. ST7	21 D1
Tomfields. ST7	21 C3
Turner Av. ST7	21 D3
Vernon Av. ST7	21 A2
Vernon Clo. ST7	21 A2
Victoria Av. ST7	21 B5
Watlands Rd. ST7	21 B1
Wedgwood Av. ST7	21 D3
Wereton Rd. ST7	21 A3
Wesley Pl. ST7	21 A5
Wesley St. ST7	21 D3
Westfield Av. ST7	21 A2
Westlands. ST7	21 C2
Wilbrahams Walk. ST7	21 A1
Wood St. ST7	21 C1
Wood Vw. ST7	21 D3
Woodcroft. ST7	21 D3
Wynbank Clo. ST7	21 B4

BIDDULPH/ BIDDULPH MOOR

Akesmore La. ST8	9 A5
Albert St. ST8	8 C4
Alders Rd. ST8	20 B5
Asquith Clo. ST8	8 E4
Baileys Bank. ST8	8 D1
Balfour Gro. ST8	8 E4
Banbury Gro. ST8	8 C4
Barmouth Clo. ST8	9 E6
Barrage Rd. ST8	20 C6
Bateman Av. ST8	9 B7
Beaumont Clo. ST8	8 D2
Beckfields Clo. ST8	20 B4
Beech Clo. ST8	20 B5
Bellringer Clo. ST8	9 C5
Birch Av. ST8	9 A6
Blackbird Way. ST8	8 E4
Bluebell Clo. ST8	9 E5
Bollin Gro. ST8	8 E3
Bomere Clo. ST8	8 C3
Brambles Ct. ST8	9 D5
Brook Gdns. ST8	8 D3
Brook St. ST8	9 A7
Broomfields. ST8	20 C5
Brown Lees Rd. ST8	9 B7
Cambridge Clo. ST8	8 C3
Carriage Dri. ST8	8 E3
Castle View. ST8	9 C6
Cecil Rd. ST8	8 C2
Cedar Gro. ST8	20 B5
Chaffinch Dri. ST8	8 E4
Chamberlain Way. ST8	8 E4
Chapel La. ST8	20 B5
Charles St. ST8	9 C5
Checkley Dri. ST8	8 D3
Chelsea Clo. ST8	8 C3
Chepstow Clo. ST8	8 C3
Cherry Tree La. ST8	20 B5
Church Clo. ST8	9 D6
Church La. ST8	20 B5
Church Rd. ST8	9 D5
Clyde Av. ST8	8 E3
Cole St. ST8	9 C5
Colwyn Dri. ST8	9 D7
Congleton Rd. ST8	8 D4
Conway Rd. ST8	9 C6
Coopers Way. ST8	8 C4
Coppice Gro. ST8	9 D5
Coracle Gro. ST8	9 E6
Cornfield Rd. ST8	9 D5
Coronation Av. ST8	9 B7
Cottage La. ST8	20 B5
Cowlishaw Clo. ST8	9 B7
Crabtree Av. ST8	9 C5
Craigside. ST8	8 C4
Crofters Clo. ST8	8 B4
Cromwell St. ST8	8 C4
Cross St. ST8	8 C4
Crossfield Av. ST8	9 C6
Crossways. ST8	8 E3
Crowborough Rd. ST8	9 F6
Dales Clo. ST8	20 C5
Dam La. ST8	20 B4
Dane Dri. ST8	8 E3
Dart Clo. ST8	8 D3
Dee Clo. ST8	8 E3
Denbigh Clo. ST8	9 C6
Derwent Dri. ST8	8 E3
Devon Gro. ST8	8 C3
Diamond Clo. ST8	8 C4
Doctors Clo. ST8	8 C4
Dorset Dri. ST8	8 C4
Douglas Av. ST8	9 D5
Dove Gro. ST8	8 D3
Duke St. ST8	9 D5
Dunnock Way. ST8	8 E4
Dylan Rd. ST8	9 E6
East Dri. ST8	8 D4
Eden Clo. ST8	8 E3
Edgeley Rd. ST8	9 D5
Edgeview Ct. ST8	9 C5
Eliases La. ST8	20 B4
Endon Dri. ST8	9 B6
Essex Dri. ST8	8 D2
Fairfield Rd. ST8	20 B5
Farmside La. ST8	20 C5
Farnham Dri. ST8	9 B7
Farnworth Clo. ST8	9 B6
Field View. ST8	8 D3
Firwood Rd. ST8	8 E3
Forge Way. ST8	9 B8
Forrester Clo. ST8	8 C4
Fountain Ct. ST8	8 D3
Gardeners Clo. ST8	9 B7
Gilbern Dri. ST8	9 B7
Gladstone Gro. ST8	8 E4
Goldcrest Way. ST8	8 E4
Grange Ct. ST8	8 D2
Grange Park Dri. ST8	8 E1
Grange Rd. ST8	8 E1
Grangefields. ST8	8 E1
Greenfield. ST8	9 D6
Greenway Rd. ST8	8 E3
Gun Battery La. ST8	20 B6
Gunn St. ST8	9 D6
Gwyn Av. ST8	9 D6
Halls La. ST8	8 C3
Halls Rd. ST8	8 C3
Hambleton Pl. ST8	9 B7
Hams Clo. ST8	9 C5
Harlech Dri. ST8	9 C6
Havelock Gro. ST8	9 C5
Hawthorn Gro. ST8	9 E5
Hazel Clo. ST8	20 B5
Healey Av. ST8	9 B7
Heath St. ST8	9 C5
Henley Av. ST8	9 A6
High St. ST8	8 C4
Highfield Pl. ST8	8 D4
Highfield Rd East. ST8	8 D4
Highfield Rd West. ST8	8 D4
Highland Clo. ST8	20 C6
Hillside Clo. ST8	20 C5
Hollytree Dri. ST8	8 C2
Holywell Clo. ST8	9 E6
Hopwood Ct. ST8	9 C5
Hot La. ST8	20 C5
Humber Dri. ST8	8 E4
Hunters Clo. ST8	8 C4
Hurst Rd. ST8	8 F1
INDUSTRIAL & RETAIL:	
Brown Lees Ind Est. ST8	9 B8
PWS Ind Est. ST8	9 B7
Ivy House Rd. ST8	8 C2
James Way. ST8	9 A6
John St. ST8	8 C4
John St. ST8	9 C5
Jubilee Clo. ST8	8 D4
Kestrel Clo. ST8	9 B6
King St. ST8	8 C4
Kingsfield Cres. ST8	8 D4
Kingsfield Rd. ST8	8 C4
Kingston Pl. ST8	8 E3
Knowle Clo. ST8	9 C5
Knype Way. ST8	9 B6
Lagonda Clo. ST8	9 B6
Lanchester Clo. ST8	9 B6
Lancia Clo. ST8	9 B6
Lask Edge Rd. ST8	20 D5
Lawton Cres. ST8	8 D4
Lawton St. ST8	8 D4
Linden Dri. ST8	8 C3
Linden Gro. ST8	8 C3
Linnet Way. ST8	8 E4
Lodge Barn Rd. ST8	9 F6
Long Valley Rd. ST8	8 C2
Lord St. ST8	9 D5
Lotus Av. ST8	9 B6
Lyndhurst Dri. ST8	9 A6
Lyneside Rd. ST8	9 B6
Lynmouth Clo. ST8	9 C6
Mansfield Dri. ST8	9 A6
Marsh Green Clo. ST8	8 D2
Marsh Gro. ST8	8 C2
Marshfield La. ST8	8 C2
Marshgreen Rd. ST8	8 C1
Mason Dri. ST8	8 B4
Mayfield Rd. ST8	9 D6
Meadowside. ST8	9 B6
Medway Dri. ST8	8 D3
Menai Dri. ST8	9 D6
Merthyr Gro. ST8	9 E6
Midfield Clo. ST8	8 C2
Mill Hayes Rd. ST8	9 C8
Minerva Clo. ST8	9 B7
Moor Clo. ST8	8 E3
Moorfield Av. ST8	8 C4
Moorland Rd. ST8	8 D4
Mossfield Dri. ST8	9 E5
Mostyn Clo. ST8	9 E6
Mow La. ST8	8 A1
Nevin Av. ST8	9 D7
New Leek La. ST8	20 A6
New St. ST8	9 F6
Newpool Rd. ST8	9 A6
Newpool Ter. ST8	9 B7
Norfolk Gro. ST8	8 C3
Northfield Dri. ST8	8 E3
Nursery Dri. ST8	8 C2
Oakdene Way. ST8	9 D5
Oakfield Gro. ST8	9 E5
Oleton Clo. ST8	9 E5
Orme Rd. ST8	9 D7
Over the Hill. ST8	20 B4
Ox-hey Cres. ST8	8 D3
Ox-hey Dri. ST8	8 D3
Palmerston Way. ST8	8 E4
Park La. ST8	9 C6
Parklands. ST8	20 C5
Pennine Way. ST8	8 E2
Pen Y Bont Walk. ST8	9 E6
Plover Dri. ST8	8 E4
Pooles Rd. ST8	20 B5
Portland Dri. ST8	8 D2
Potters End. ST8	8 C3
Princess St. ST8	9 D5
Queens Dri. ST8	9 D6
Redwing Dri. ST8	8 E4
Ribble Dri. ST8	8 E3
Ridgefields. ST8	20 C5
Robin Hill. ST8	20 A6
Rosebery Clo. ST8	8 E4
Rowan Clo. ST8	20 B6
Royce Av. ST8	9 B7
Ruabon Clo. ST8	9 E6
Rudyard Rd. ST8	20 C5
Rupert St. ST8	8 C4
Ruthin Gro. ST8	9 E6
St Davids Way. ST8	9 E6
St Johns Pl. ST8	9 C5
St Johns Rd. ST8	9 C5
Salter St. ST8	9 C5
Sandsdown Clo. ST8	8 C3
Sandy Rd. ST8	8 C2
Sawyer Dri. ST8	8 C3
School La. ST8	20 B4
Severn Clo. ST8	8 E4
Shakespeare Ct. ST8	9 C5
Shaw St. ST8	9 C5
Shepherd St. ST8	9 C5
Silver Clo. ST8	8 C4
Smithy La. ST8	8 D2
Smokies Way. ST8	8 C3
South View. ST8	8 C4
Spedding Way. ST8	8 E4
Springfield Gro. ST8	9 D5
Springfield Rd. ST8	9 D5
Squirrel Hayes Av. ST8	9 E6
Stanley Rd. ST8	8 C2
Stanley St. ST8	8 C4
Stanways La. ST8	20 C4
Station Rd. ST8	8 C3
Stoneyfields. ST8	20 B5
Style Clo. ST8	9 B7
Swallow Walk. ST8	8 E4
Swift Dri. ST8	8 E4
Sycamore Clo. ST8	8 E2
Tame Clo. ST8	8 D3
Tay Clo. ST8	8 E3
Tern Clo. ST8	8 E4
Thames Dri. ST8	8 D3
Thatcher Gro. ST8	8 B4
The Uplands. ST8	8 E2
Thomas St. ST8	8 D4
Top Rd. ST8	20 D5
Torville Dri. ST8	9 B6
Tower Clo. ST8	9 B6
Tower Hill Rd. ST8	9 A6
Trent Gro. ST8	9 D6
Trentley Dri. ST8	20 C6
Tunstall Rd. ST8	9 B6
Turnlea Clo. ST8	20 B6
Under the Hill. ST8	20 B5
Victoria Row. ST8	9 C8
Villa Clo. ST8	9 C5
Walley St. ST8	8 C4
Warwick St. ST8	9 C5
Washington Clo. ST8	8 C3
Weaver Clo. ST8	8 D3
Wedgwood La. ST8	8 C2
Well La. ST8	8 C2
Well St. ST8	8 C4
Wells Clo. ST8	8 D4
West St. ST8	9 C5
Wharf Rd. ST8	8 C4
Whetstone Rd. ST8	8 C2
Whitbread Dri. ST8	8 E4
Wickenstones Ct. ST8	9 D5
William Av. ST8	9 D5
Willow Pl. ST8	20 B5
Witham Way. ST8	8 E3
Woodhouse La, Biddulph. ST8	8 D2
Woodhouse La, Biddulph Moor. ST8	20 B5
Woodland St. ST8	9 D5
Wraggs La. ST8	20 C5
Wrexham Clo. ST8	8 D3
York Clo. ST8	8 D2

KIDSGROVE

Acacia Gdns. ST7	15 F1
Acres Nook Rd. ST6	14 D5
Albany St. ST6	15 F5
Alder Clo. ST7	15 E4
Alderhay La. ST7	13 G5
Alice St. ST6	15 G5
Alma Clo. ST7	12 B3
Ancaster St. ST6	15 G5
Andrew St. ST6	15 G4
Anne Ct. ST7	14 B6
Anne St. ST6	15 G5
Ashenough Rd. ST7	14 B6
Aspen Clo. ST7	13 H6
Astbury Clo. ST7	15 G2
Attwood St. ST7	15 E2
Aubrey St. ST6	15 F5
Audley Rd. ST7	14 A5
Avon Clo. ST7	15 F2
Back Heathcote St. ST7	14 D2
Banbury St. ST7	14 B3
Bank St. ST7	13 F6
Barber Dri. ST7	12 C3
Barleycroft Ter. ST7	12 C2
Barnbridge Clo. ST7	12 C2
Barrie Gdns. ST7	14 A4
Bedford Rd. ST7	14 D1
Beech Dri. ST7	14 C4
Beeston View. ST7	15 E5
Bevan Av. ST7	14 B6
Biddulph Rd. ST7	11 H4
Birch Tree La. ST7	13 E2
Birchall Av. ST6	15 F6
Birches Way. ST7	15 F2
Birkdale Dri. ST7	15 G1
Bishops Clo. ST7	14 B4
Boat Horse Rd. ST7	14 D3
Boat Horse Rd, Ravenscliffe. ST6	15 E6
Bosley Gro. ST6	15 G5

Bourne Rd. ST7 14 D2
Bourne St. ST7 13 G3
Brake Village. ST7 13 F3
Brakespeare St. ST6 15 G5
Brieryhurst Rd. ST7 15 F1
Brights Av. ST7 15 F2
Brindley Clo. ST7 14 B3
Broadfield Rd. ST6 15 E5
Browning Gro. ST7 14 A4
Bullocks Ho Rd. ST7 11 H6
Burnaby Rd. ST6 15 G6
Burns Clo. ST7 14 D4
Burnwood Gro. ST7 15 F2
Butt La. ST7 14 B2
Byron Ct. ST7 14 D4
Capper Clo. ST7 15 E2
Cartlich St. ST6 15 G6
Castle Rd. ST7 13 H2
Castle View Rd. ST7 15 F1
Cedar Av. ST7 14 B3
Central St. ST7 13 F3
Chapel Bank. ST7 13 G3
Chapel Clo. ST7 13 F4
Chapel La. ST7 13 H6
Chapel St,
  Church Lawton. ST7 14 B2
Chapel St,
  Mow Cop. ST7 13 F3
Charlotte St. ST6 15 F4
Charnwood. ST7 15 E2
Chatterley Dri. ST7 15 E5
Chester Clo. ST7 14 B5
Chester Rd. ST7 14 B5
Church La,
  Mow Cop. ST7 13 H3
Church La,
  Scholar Grn. ST7 12 A1
Church St,
  Church Lawton. ST7 14 A2
Church St,
  Mow Cop. ST7 13 F4
Church St,
  The Rookery. ST7 13 F6
Cinderhill La. ST7 12 C3
Clare St,
  Harriseahead. ST7 13 H6
Clare St, Mow Cop. ST7 13 F4
Close La. ST7 13 G2
Clough Hall Dri. ST7 14 C5
Clough Hall Rd. ST7 14 C4
Coalpit Hill. ST7 14 B4
Cob Moor Rd. ST7 12 D5
Colclough La. ST6 15 G5
Collinson Rd. ST6 15 G5
Congleton Rd,
  Butt Lane. ST7 14 B3
Congleton Rd,
  Mow Cop. ST7 13 H2
Congleton Rd,
  Scholar Grn. ST7 12 C1
Congleton Rd Nth. ST7 12 C3
Congleton Rd Sth. ST7 14 B1
Coppice Rd. ST7 14 A4
Coronation Cres. ST7 14 C3
Cotton Rd. ST6 15 F5
Covert Gdns. ST7 14 B4
Crown Bank. ST7 14 B5
Crown Bank Cres. ST7 14 B5
Crown Gdns. ST7 14 B6
Cumberland Clo. ST7 14 C4
Dales Grn Rd. ST7 13 G4
Dane Gdns. ST7 15 G2
Dee Clo. ST7 14 B5
Derby Rd. ST7 14 B5
Derwent Cres. ST7 15 G2
Diglake Clo. ST7 14 A6
Dorchester Clo. ST7 15 E1
Dorset Pl. ST7 15 E1
Dovedale Clo. ST6 15 F5
Drenfell Rd. ST7 12 C2
Drumber La. ST7 13 E1
Drummond St. ST6 15 G5
Edale Clo. ST6 15 F5
Eden Clo. ST7 15 E2
Elgood La. ST6 15 F5
Elizabeth Ct. ST7 14 B6
Elm Clo. ST7 15 E4
Elton Ter. ST6 15 G5
Essex Dri. ST7 14 D2
Everest Rd. ST7 15 F1
Fawfield Dri. ST6 15 G5

Ferney Pl. ST6 15 G5
Fifth Av. ST7 14 C3
Fir Clo. ST7 13 G2
First Av. ST7 14 C3
Fords La. ST7 13 G2
Foundry La. ST7 12 D2
Fourth Av. ST7 14 C3
Fox Gdns. ST7 14 B4
Galleys Bank. ST7 15 E1
Garbett St. ST6 15 G5
Gilbert Clo. ST7 15 E2
Gilbert St. ST6 15 F5
Gill Bank Rd. ST7 15 E5
Gillbank Rd. ST7 15 E4
Glebe St. ST7 14 B2
Gloucester Rd. ST7 14 C2
Golf Links Clo. ST6 15 G4
Gordon Rd. ST6 15 G6
Grays Clo. ST7 13 E2
Greenside Clo. ST7 14 D4
Grove Av. ST7 14 C3
Hall Rd. ST7 13 F3
Hardings Wood. ST7 14 C2
Hardingswood Rd. ST7 14 C2
Harecastle Av. ST7 14 B3
Harriseahead La. ST7 13 G5
Hawthorns Gdns. ST7 14 B4
Hayhead Clo. ST7 15 F2
Hazel Clo. ST7 15 F1
Heath St. ST6 15 G5
Heathcote St. ST7 14 D2
*Heathfield Ct,
  Heath St. ST6 15 G5
Heathside La. ST6 15 F5
Henshall Pl. ST6 15 F5
High St, Goldenhill. ST6 15 F5
High St,
  Harriseahead. ST7 13 H5
High St, Mow Cop. ST7 13 G3
High St,
  Newchapel. ST7 15 H1
High St, Talke Pits. ST7 14 B6
High St,
  The Rookery. ST7 13 F6
High View. ST7 13 F4
Higher Ash Rd. ST7 14 B3
Highfield Av. ST7 15 E2
Hilary Rd. ST7 15 F1
Hillside Av. ST7 15 E4
Hillside Clo. ST7 13 G3
Holehouse La. ST7 12 A2
Hollins Cres. ST7 14 B3
Hollins Grange. ST7 14 B3
Hollinshead Clo. ST7 12 D2
Hollinwood Clo. ST7 14 C4
Hollinwood Rd. ST7 14 C4
Holly La. ST7 13 H4
Hollywall La. ST6 15 F6
Hulton Clo. ST7 14 B6
Ian Rd. ST7 15 G1

INDUSTRIAL & RETAIL:
Freeport Shopping Mall,
  ST7 14 A6
  Hardingwood Ind Est. ST7 14 C2
  Jamage Ind Est. ST7 14 A6
  Linley Trading Est. ST7 14 A3
  Nelson Ind Est. ST7 14 A3
Jamage Rd. ST7 14 B6
Jasmine Cres. ST7 15 H1
Jodrell View. ST7 15 E4
Joseph St. ST6 15 G5
Keats Gdns. ST7 14 D4
Kidsgrove Bank. ST7 15 F3
Kidsgrove Rd. ST6 15 F4
King St, Kidsgrove. ST7 14 D2
King St, Talke Pits. ST7 14 B6
Kingsley Clo. ST7 14 B6
Kingsley Rd. ST7 14 B6
Kingswood. ST7 15 E3
Kinnersley Av. ST7 14 C4
Kinnersley St. ST7 15 E2
Kite Gro. ST7 15 G1
Knowsley La. ST7 12 B6
Laburnam Clo. ST7 14 C4
Lamb St. ST7 14 D2
Lapwing Gro. ST7 15 G1
Larch Clo. ST7 15 E4
Lark Av. ST7 15 G1
Larkfield. ST7 15 E2
Latebrook Clo. ST6 15 F5
Laurel Dri. ST7 13 H6

Lawton Av. ST7 14 B1
Lawton Coppice. ST7 12 B5
Lawton St. ST7 13 F6
Lewisham Dri. ST6 15 F5
Lichfield Rd. ST7 14 B5
Lime Kiln La. ST7 14 C1
Lincoln Rd. ST7 14 D2
Linley Rd. ST7 14 A3
Little Bleeding. ST7 12 C5
Little Moss Clo. ST7 12 C5
Little Moss La. ST7 12 C5
Liverpool Rd. ST7 14 D2
Liverpool Rd East. ST7 14 A1
Liverpool Rd West. ST7 14 A1
Lodge Rd. ST7 14 B6
Long La. ST7 13 H6
Long Row. ST7 14 D3
Lower Ash Rd. ST7 14 B4
Lynn Av. ST7 14 A4
Magpie Cres. ST7 15 F2
Manor Rd. ST7 13 G2
Maple Av. ST7 14 B3
Margery Av. ST7 12 C3
Market St. ST7 15 E2
Marldon Pl. ST6 15 G6
Marsh Av. ST6 15 H2
Maureen Av. ST6 15 G5
Mead Av. ST7 12 C3
Meadow Ct. ST7 15 H2
Meadows Rd. ST7 14 D2
Meadowside La. ST7 13 E2
Medina Way. ST7 15 E2
Mellors Bank. ST7 13 G4
Merelake Rd. ST7 14 A4
Merlin Av. ST7 15 G1
Mill Gro. ST7 14 B3
Mill La. ST7 13 E2
Mill Rise. ST7 14 D3
Millers View. ST7 14 D3
Millstone Av. ST7 14 B2
Milton Cres. ST7 14 A4
Minfield Clo. ST7 15 E4
Mistley Walk. ST6 15 F4
Mitchell Av. ST7 14 B3
Mitchell Dri. ST7 14 B3
Mobberley Rd. ST6 15 F4
Monument Rd. ST7 14 B6
Moorland Rd. ST7 13 H3
Moorson Av. ST7 15 D2
Moreton Clo. ST7 15 E4
Moreton Pl. ST7 12 B3
Moss La. ST7 12 C5
Moss Pl. ST7 15 E1
Mossfield Cres. ST7 15 E3
Mount Pleasant. ST7 15 E3
Mount Pleasant Rd. ST7 13 E2
Mount Rd. ST7 15 E2
Mow Cop Rd. ST7 13 F4
Mow La. ST7 13 E5
Murray St. ST7 15 G5
Nabbswood Rd. ST7 15 F2
Napier Gdns. ST7 15 E2
Nelson Bank. ST6 14 D4
Newark Gro. ST6 15 G5
Newcastle Rd. ST7 14 B4
Newchapel Rd. ST7 13 E6
Norfolk Rd. ST7 14 D2
North St. ST7 13 F4
Nursery Clo. ST7 14 B3
Nursery Rd. ST7 12 C4
Oak Dri. ST7 12 B3
Old Butt La. ST7 14 A2
Old School Clo. ST7 14 D3
Oldcott Cres. ST7 15 F4
Oldcott Dri. ST7 15 F4
Oldhill Clo. ST7 14 B3
Orchard Cres. ST7 14 B3
Osprey View. ST7 15 G1
Park Av. ST7 14 C4
Park Farm View. ST6 15 G5
Park View Rd. ST7 15 E1
Parklands. ST7 15 E2
Peakdale Av. ST6 15 F5
Peckforton View. ST7 15 E4
Pennyfields Rd. ST7 15 G1
Perkins St. ST6 15 F5
Phoenix Clo. ST7 15 G1
Pickwick Pl. ST7 14 B2
Pine Clo. ST7 14 A5
Pit La. ST7 14 A6
Poplar Dri. ST7 15 E3

Portland Dri. ST7 12 C3
Powy Dri. ST7 15 E2
Premier Gdns. ST7 14 D2
Primitive St. ST7 13 G3
Princess St. ST7 14 B6
Priory Pl. ST7 15 F1
Quarry Ter. ST7 15 E3
Queen St. ST7 14 D2
Queens Gdns. ST7 14 B6
Randel La. ST6 15 F4
Ravenscliffe Rd. ST7 14 D4
Rectory Gdns. ST7 14 B5
Rectory View. ST7 14 B5
Red Lion Clo. ST7 14 B4
Regency Clo. ST7 14 B6
Ridge Rd. ST6 15 G6
Rigby Rd. ST7 13 F6
Rockhouse La. ST7 14 A4
Rockside. ST7 13 G3
Rodgers St. ST6 15 F4
Rookery Rd. ST7 15 F1
Rowan Clo. ST7 15 E4
Russell Pl. ST6 15 H6
Russell Rd. ST6 15 H6
Rutland Rd. ST7 15 E1
St Andrews Dri. ST7 15 F1
St Johns Wood. ST7 14 D3
St Martins Rd. ST7 14 B6
St Saviours St. ST7 14 B3
St Thomas St. ST7 13 H3
Salop Pl. ST7 15 E1
Sands Rd. ST7 13 H3
Sandy Rd. ST6 15 G5
Second Av. ST7 14 C3
Shakespeare Clo. ST7 14 D3
Shannon Dri. ST6 15 F4
Shelford Rd. ST6 15 G6
Shelley Clo. ST7 15 D4
Silvermine Clo. ST7 15 F2
Silverwood. ST7 15 F2
Skellern St. ST7 14 B2
Slacken La. ST7 14 B2
Sneyd Pl. ST6 15 G6
Somerset Av. ST7 14 D2
South St. ST7 13 F4
Sparrowbutts Gro. ST7 15 F2
Spey Dri. ST7 15 F1
Spout Hollow. ST7 14 B6
Springbank. ST7 12 D2
Springfield Dri. ST 14 B4
Springhead Clo. ST7 14 B6
Starling Clo. ST7 15 G1
Station Rd,
  Kidsgrove. ST7 14 D2
Station Rd,
  Mow Cop. ST7 13 F2
Station Rd,
  Newchapel. ST7 15 H2
Station Rd,
  Scholar Grn. ST7 12 C2
Stone Bank Rd. ST7 15 E3
Stone Chair La. ST7 12 C2
Summerfield. ST7 15 E3
Surrey Rd. ST7 15 E2
Sussex Dri. ST7 14 D1
Swallow Clo. ST7 15 G1
Swallowmore Vw. ST7 14 A4
Swan Bank. ST7 14 A5
Swan Clo. ST7 14 B4
Swift Clo. ST7 15 E2
Sycamore Clo. ST7 14 C4
Tamar Rd. ST7 15 E2
Target Clo. ST7 14 B6
Tawney Clo. ST7 15 F1
Taylor St. ST6 15 G5
Telford Clo. ST7 14 C3
Temperance Pl. ST6 15 G5
Tennyson Av. ST7 14 D4
Tern Av. ST7 15 G2
The Avenue. ST7 14 D3
The Bank. ST7 13 E2
The Brake. ST7 13 F3
*The Hollins,
  Congleton Rd. ST7 14 B3
The Hollow. ST7 13 F4
The Mount,
  Kidsgrove. ST7 15 E3
The Mount,
  Scholar Grn. ST7 12 C3
The Spinney. ST7 12 B5
The Views. ST7 15 H2

64

Street	Ref
Ashwell Rd. ST4	40 A4
Ashwood. ST3	49 E2
Ashwood Gro. ST11	60 E3
Ashwood Ter. ST3	49 E2
Ashworth St. ST4	47 H1
Askern Clo. ST3	56 A1
Aster Clo. ST3	50 D1
Aston Rd. ST5	22 A4
Astro Gro. ST3	48 D4
Athelstan St. ST6	24 A1
Athena Rd. ST1	32 B3
Atherstone Rd. ST4	52 D4
Athlone St. ST6	25 H4
Atholl Rd. ST3	55 G1
Atlam Clo. ST2	32 C6
Atlantic Gro. ST4	53 F2
Atlas St. ST4	48 A2
Auckland St. ST6	24 D6
Auden Pl. ST3	49 G4
Audley Pl. ST5	45 F1
Audley Rd. ST5	22 A4
Audley St, Knutton. ST5	38 C1
Audley St, Tunstall. ST6	24 A2
Austin St. ST1	42 A2
Austwick Gro. ST1	46 B2
Aveling Grn. ST1	26 B6
Aveling Rd. ST1	26 B6
Avenue Rd. ST4	41 F3
Avion Clo. ST3	57 E4
Avoca St. ST1	31 H3
Avon Clo. ST5	45 F4
Avondale St. ST6	24 A6
Avonside Av. ST6	16 D6
Avonwick Gro. ST1	32 C3
Axon Cres. ST3	50 D4
Aylesbury Rd. ST2	43 E1
Aynsley Av. ST5	45 G4
Aynsley Rd. ST4	41 E3
Aynsleys Dri. ST11	57 G4
Ayrshire Gro. ST3	55 F2
Ayshford St. ST3	49 E5
Back Bunts La. ST9	27 G1
Back Ford Grn Rd. ST6	25 G3
Back La, Brown Edge. ST6	19 E3
Back La, Hill Top. ST6	19 E1
Baddeley Green La. ST2	27 E4
Baddeley Hall Rd. ST2	27 F3
Baddeley Rd. ST2	27 E4
Baddeley St. ST6	24 D5
Baden Rd. ST6	25 G4
Baden St. ST5	39 F2
Badger Gro. ST3	57 E4
Badgers Brow. ST1	32 B6
Baggott Pl. ST5	38 D4
Bagnall Rd. ST2	27 E5
Bagnall St. ST1	6 B4
Bagot Gro. ST1	26 B6
Bailey Rd. ST3	48 B3
Bailey St, Cliff Vale. ST4	40 C2
Bailey St, Newcastle. ST5	39 F3
Bainbridge Rd. ST4	52 D4
Bains Gro. ST3	23 E6
Baker Cres. ST2	27 E2
Baker Cres Nth. ST2	27 E2
Baker Cres Sth. ST2	27 E3
Baker St. ST4	48 A1
Bakewell Clo. ST5	37 G3
Balcombe Clo. ST5	39 F5
Balfour St. ST1	31 H6
Ball Green La. ST6	18 A5
Ball Hayes Rd. ST6	17 F6
Ball La. ST6	18 C6
Ballinson Rd. ST3	48 B6
Balloon St. ST4	40 A3
Balls Yard. ST5	39 G3
Balmoral Clo. ST4	46 D6
Baltic Clo. ST4	53 F3
Bamber Pl. ST5	29 E2
Bamber St. ST4	41 E5
Bambury St. ST3	49 F1
Bamford Gro. ST3	31 F4
Bancroft La. ST11	60 D3
Bank Hall Rd. ST6	25 F3
Bank House Dri. ST5	40 B2
Bank St. ST6	24 A1
Bankfield Rd. ST3	56 A2
Bankhouse Rd, Forsbrook. ST11	60 F2
Bankhouse Rd, Trentham. ST4	52 C2
Bankside. ST5	39 H4
Banksman Rd. ST2	43 G6
Banktop Av. ST6	25 E2
Banky Brook Clo. ST6	25 F2
Bannister Clo. ST4	47 E3
Baptist St. ST6	24 D6
Barber Pl. ST6	16 D4
Barber Rd. ST6	16 D4
Barber St. ST6	24 C4
Barbridge Rd. ST5	22 B4
Barclay St. ST3	49 E2
Bardsey Walk. ST3	48 C4
Barford Rd. ST5	45 E4
Barford St. ST3	49 E4
Bargrave Dri. ST5	23 G5
Bargrave St. ST2	43 G3
Barker St, Broad Meadow. ST5	28 D3
Barker St, Longton. ST6	49 F5
Barkers Sq. ST5	30 A4
Barks Dri. ST6	17 H6
Barlaston Old Rd. ST4	53 E5
Barlaston Rd. ST3	54 C2
Barleyfields. ST6	25 F2
Barleyford Dri. ST3	49 G1
Barlow St. ST3	49 F5
Barlstone Av. ST11	60 D3
Barn Ct. ST6	45 G5
Barncroft Rd. ST6	17 F5
Barnes Way. ST3	55 E2
Barnett Gro. ST6	16 C6
Barnfield. ST4	46 C2
Barnfield Rd. ST6	30 D1
Barnlea Gro. ST3	56 C6
Barnsdale Clo. ST4	58 D1
Barnwell Gro. ST4	52 D1
Barracks St. ST3	39 G4
Barratt Gdns. ST2	27 E5
Barratt Cres. ST3	31 E3
Barratt Dri. ST6	30 D2
Barrington Ct. ST5	30 B6
Barry Av. ST2	32 C6
Bartholomew Rd. ST3	56 A2
Barthomley Rd. ST1	31 H2
Bartlem St. ST3	49 G2
Barton Cres. ST6	24 B4
Basford Park Rd. ST5	40 A1
Baskerville Rd. ST1	31 H4
Baskeyfield Pl. ST6	17 F5
Basnetts Wood Rd. ST9	20 A3
Bassilow Rd. ST4	42 B6
Bath Rd. ST6	37 E1
Bath St, Stoke. ST4	41 E6
Bath St, Weston Coyney. ST3	50 D2
Bath Ter. ST4	41 E6
Baths Pas. ST3	49 E4
Baths Rd. ST3	49 E3
Bathurst St. ST3	49 F4
Batkin Clo. ST6	17 F5
Batten Ct. ST3	57 E4
Battison Cres. ST3	49 E6
Bay Tree Clo. ST1	32 B3
Bayham Walk. ST3	32 D5
Beaconsfield. ST5	29 G2
Beaconsfield Dri. ST3	54 A2
Beadnell Gro. ST3	55 F1
Beard Gro. ST2	32 D1
Beasley Av. ST5	28 D2
Beasley Pl. ST5	28 D1
Beata Rd. ST5	22 D4
Beatrice Clo. ST4	47 E6
Beattie Av. ST3	39 G1
Beaufort Av. ST9	34 C5
Beaufort Rd. ST3	49 F5
Beaulieu Clo. ST9	34 D6
Beaumaris Clo. ST4	40 A4
Beaumaris Ct. ST5	39 E5
Beaumont Rd. ST6	24 B2
Beaver Clo. ST4	46 B3
Beckenham Clo. ST3	57 E4
Beckett Av. ST3	56 D1
Beckford St. ST1	31 H4
Beckton Av. ST6	24 C2
Bedale Pl. ST3	54 A1
Bedcroft. ST12	59 H4
Beddow Way. ST6	16 C4
Bedford Cres. ST5	45 G3
Bedford Rd. ST1	41 E2
Beech Dale Rd. ST4	58 A6
Beech Gro. ST4	47 G3
Beech Rd. ST3	48 B6
Beech St. ST3	49 F4
Beechcliff La. ST12	58 A4
Beechcroft. ST12	59 H4
Beeches Row. ST6	16 A5
Beechfield Rd. ST4	53 F5
Beechfields. ST12	59 H3
Beechmont Gro. ST1	32 B3
Beechwood Clo, Blythe Bridge. ST11	60 D3
Beechwood Clo, Westbury Park. ST5	44 B5
Beeston St. ST3	49 F2
Belfast Clo. ST6	25 F3
Belfield Av. ST5	29 H5
Belford Pl. ST4	40 C3
Belgrave Av. ST3	49 E6
Belgrave Cres. ST3	55 F1
Belgrave Rd, Florence. ST3	49 E6
Belgrave Rd, Newcastle. ST5	39 H4
Bell Av. ST3	49 G5
Bell La. ST12	59 G1
Bellerton La. ST6	26 A3
Bellingham Gro. ST1	31 H2
Bellringer Rd. ST4	53 H3
Bells Hollow. ST5	22 B3
Bellwood Clo. ST3	56 C5
Belmont Rd. ST1	40 D1
Belsay Clo. ST3	49 E3
Belvedere Rd. ST4	52 D1
Belvoir Av. ST4	53 F6
Bemersley Rd. ST6	17 H1
Benedict St. ST2	32 D4
Benfleet Pl. ST3	48 D5
Bengal Gro. ST4	53 F2
Bengry Rd. ST3	49 H6
Bennet Precinct. ST3	49 E4
Bennett St. ST6	29 G1
Bennett St. ST3	30 C1
Bennion St. ST3	49 F5
Benson St. ST6	16 C5
Bentley Av. ST5	29 F5
Bentley Rd. ST6	17 G5
Berdmore St. ST4	48 D2
Beresford Cres. ST5	45 E1
Beresford St. ST4	41 F3
Bergamot Dri. ST3	56 C5
Berkeley St. ST1	6 D6
Bernard Gro. ST3	55 F5
Bernard St. ST1	6 D6
Berne Av. ST3	38 C6
Berry Hill Rd. ST4	41 H3
Berry Hill Rd. ST4	42 B3
Berry La. ST3	49 E4
Berry St. ST4	41 E5
Berryfield Gro. ST3	50 B4
Berwick Rd. ST1	26 A5
Berwick Walks. ST5	38 D5
Best St. ST4	48 C1
Beswick Rd. ST6	16 D5
Bethel St. ST1	25 G6
Bethesda Rd. ST1	41 G2
Bethesda St. ST1	6 B5
Betley Pl. ST5	45 H1
Bettany Rd. ST6	31 E1
Bevandean Clo. ST4	53 G6
Beveridge Clo. ST3	50 D6
Beverley Cres. ST11	60 E2
Beverley Dri. ST2	43 E1
Beville St. ST4	42 B6
Bevin La. ST2	32 D6
Bew St. ST6	18 A5
Bewcastle Gro. ST3	56 C3
Bexhill Gro. ST1	32 C3
Bexley St. ST1	6 A1
Biddulph Rd. ST6	16 D4
Billinge St. ST6	24 C6
Bilton St. ST4	47 E1
Birch Green Gro. ST1	32 A2
Birch Gro, Forsbrook. ST11	60 E2
Birch Gro, Meir Heath. ST3	55 G6
Birch House Rd. ST5	22 B6
Birch St. ST3	32 A4
Birch Ter. ST1	6 C5
Birch Walk. ST3	54 C1
Bircham Walk. ST5	45 F6
Birchdown Av. ST6	25 E2
Birchenwood Rd. ST6	16 B2
Birches Head Rd. ST1	31 H3
Birchfield Rd. ST2	33 F3
Birchgate. ST2	33 F5
Birchgate Gro. ST2	33 F5
Birchlands Rd. ST1	32 B3
Birchover Walk. ST6	17 E2
Bird Cage Walk. ST1	6 B4
Bird Rd. ST3	50 C5
Birkholme Dri. ST3	55 G4
Birks St. ST4	47 F2
Birrell St. ST4	48 C2
Biscay Gro. ST4	53 F2
Bishop Rd. ST6	17 E5
Bishop St. ST4	48 C2
Bitterne Pl. ST2	43 G4
Black Horse La. ST1	6 A3
Blackbank Rd. ST5	38 A1
Blackbird Way. ST6	16 C1
Blackbrook Av. ST5	22 A5
Blackfriars Rd. ST5	39 F4
Blackheath Clo. ST3	49 G5
Blackhorse La. ST1	31 F5
Blacklake Dri. ST3	55 G5
Blackthorn Pl. ST5	22 C5
Blackwells Row. ST6	31 F3
Blackwood Pl. ST3	50 A3
Bladon Av. ST5	45 G5
Bladon Clo. ST5	17 E2
Blake St. ST6	24 C6
Blakelow Rd. ST2	32 D3
Blakeney Av. ST5	45 G5
Blanchard Clo. ST3	57 E4
Blantyre St. ST3	49 E6
Blatchford Clo. ST3	50 D6
Bleak Pl. ST6	31 E1
Bleak St. ST5	30 A6
Bleakridge Av. ST5	23 G6
Blencarn Gro. ST9	27 F1
Blenheim St. ST4	47 H2
Bleriot Clo. ST3	57 E4
Blithfield Clo. ST9	34 C6
Bluebell Dri. ST5	45 E3
Bluestone Av. ST6	25 F4
Blunt St. ST5	29 H5
Blurton Priory. ST4	54 C2
Blurton Rd, Hollybush. ST3	48 A3
Blurton Rd, Newstead. ST4	54 C5
Blythe Av. ST3	55 G4
Blythe Bridge Rd. ST11	60 C1
Blythe Clo. ST11	57 F3
Blythe Mount Pk. ST11	60 E2
Blythe Rd. ST11	60 E2
Blythe View. ST11	60 D3
Bogs La. ST11	60 D3
Bolberry Clo. ST3	56 A1
Bold St. ST1	32 A4
Bolina Gro. ST3	43 E6
Bolney Gro. ST1	32 C3
Bolsover Clo. ST6	16 D2
Bolton Pl. ST3	56 B2
Boma Rd. ST4	52 C3
Bond St. ST6	16 A6
Bondfield Way. ST6	50 D5
Bonnard Clo. ST3	57 E4
Bonner Clo. ST4	46 B3
Boon Av. ST4	40 D6
Booth St, Broad Meadow. ST5	28 D3
Booth St, Stoke. ST4	47 E1
Boothen Grn. ST4	47 E2
Boothen Old Rd. ST4	47 F2
Boothen Rd. ST4	47 F1
Boothenwood Ter. ST4	46 D2
Boothroyd St. ST6	6 C5
Bordeaux Clo. ST3	56 C3
Bordeaux Wk. ST5	44 D4
Borough Rd. ST5	39 H3
Borrowdale Rd. ST6	26 A2
Boscombe Gro. ST4	59 E1

Bosinney Clo. ST4	49 E2
Boston Clo. ST6	23 H1
Boswell St. ST4	40 C2
Botany Bay Rd. ST1	32 A4
Botesworth Gdns. ST6	24 A5
Botteslow St. ST1	6 D5
Boughey Rd. ST4	41 G4
Boughey St. ST4	47 E1
Boulton St, Dimsdale. ST5	29 H3
Boulton St, Hanley. ST1	31 H3
Boundary Ct. ST1	6 B1
Boundary St, Hanley. ST1	31 F4
Boundary St, Newcastle. ST5	40 A3
Bourne St. ST4	48 A3
Bournes Bank. ST6	24 D6
Bouverie Par. ST1	26 B6
Bow St. ST1	6 C1
Bowden St. ST6	25 E4
Bower St. ST1	41 G2
Bowfell Gro. ST3	43 E6
Bowland Av. ST5	38 C1
Bowlers Clo. ST6	31 E3
Bowman Gro. ST6	17 F2
Bowmead Clo. ST4	53 G4
Bowness St. ST1	31 F3
Bowstead St. ST4	41 F6
Bowyer Av. ST6	18 A5
Box La. ST3	50 B5
Boxwood Pl. ST5	22 B5
Brabazon Clo. ST3	57 E4
Bracken Clo, Meir Heath. ST5	55 F5
Bracken Clo, Tittensor. ST12	58 B6
Bracken St. ST4	48 B3
Brackenberry. ST5	39 G1
Brackenfield Av. ST2	43 F3
Brackley Av. ST4	25 F4
Bradbury Clo. ST6	26 B2
Bradford Ter. ST1	32 A3
Bradley Village. ST6	25 F2
Bradwell Grange. ST5	29 G2
Bradwell La. ST5	29 E1
Bradwell Lodge. ST5	29 G2
Bradwell St. ST6	24 A6
Braemar Clo. ST2	33 G6
Braemore Rd. ST2	33 E2
Braithwell Dri. ST2	26 D3
Bramfield Dri. ST5	39 G2
Bramley Pl. ST4	46 B5
Brammall Dri. ST11	57 G4
Brammer St. ST6	25 F2
Brampton Clo. ST9	20 B1
Brampton Gdns. ST5	39 H1
Brampton Rd. ST5	39 H2
Brampton Sidings. ST5	39 G2
Brandon Gro. ST4	52 C2
Branson Av. ST3	49 H4
Bransty Gro. ST4	53 G6
Brant Av. ST5	29 F5
Brassington Way. ST2	43 F2
Brattice Pl. ST2	43 G6
Braystones Clo. ST6	16 C2
Breach Rd. ST6	19 F3
Bream Way. ST6	25 F3
Brecon Way. ST2	43 F2
Breedon Clo. ST5	28 D6
Breeze Av. ST6	16 B6
Brendale Clo. ST4	46 D6
Brentnor Clo. ST3	50 A5
Brentwood Ct. ST9	34 D4
Brentwood Dri. ST9	34 D4
Brentwood Gro, Stockton Brook. ST9	27 F2
Brentwood Gro, Werrington. ST9	34 D4
Brereton Pl. ST6	24 B5
Bretherton Pl. ST6	16 D4
Brewery St. ST1	6 B1
Brewester Rd. ST2	42 C1
Brianson Av. ST4	31 G1
Briarbank Clo. ST4	52 C1
Briarswood Pl. ST3	50 D6
Brick Kiln La. ST5	28 C1
Brickfield Pl. ST3	49 F1
Brickhouse St. ST6	24 D6
Brickkiln La. ST4	40 C2

Bridestowe Clo. ST3	56 C3
Bridge Rd. ST4	45 B5
Bridge St, Newcastle. ST5	39 F3
Bridge St, Silverdale. ST5	38 A2
Bridgecroft. ST6	17 F4
Bridgett Clo. ST4	46 B2
Bridgewater St. ST6	24 A6
Bridgewood St. ST3	49 F4
Bridgnorth Gro. ST5	22 C3
Bridgwood Rd. ST11	60 E2
Bridle Pth. ST2	34 B5
Brierley St. ST6	25 G4
Brieryhurst Clo. ST2	33 F3
Bright St. ST3	56 C1
Brightgreen St. ST3	49 G1
Brighton St. ST4	40 D5
Brindiwell Gro. ST4	53 G4
Brindley La. ST9	27 F3
Brindley Pl. ST6	17 F4
Brindley St. ST5	39 F3
Brindon Clo. ST3	50 D4
Brinsley Av. ST4	52 D4
Brisley Hill. ST4	46 D1
Bristol St. ST5	30 A4
Brittain Av. ST3	28 D1
Brittle Pl. ST4	25 H3
Britton St. ST4	40 C3
Brixham Clo. ST2	42 C3
Broad La. ST6	19 E1
Broad Meadow Ct. ST5	28 D2
Broad St, Newcastle. ST5	39 F3
Broad St, Stoke. ST4	6 A5
Broadhurst St. ST6	25 E4
Broadmans Bank. ST6	18 D1
Broadmine St. ST4	42 B6
Broadoak Way. ST3	54 A2
Broadway. ST3	50 B6
Broadway Ct. ST3	56 B1
Broadway Pl. ST3	50 B6
Brockbank Pl. ST6	17 E5
Brocklehurst Way. ST1	32 A1
Brockley Sq. ST1	6 B3
Brocksford St. ST4	48 D2
Brockton Walk. ST3	54 A1
Brogan St. ST4	48 B1
Bromford Pl. ST1	41 E1
Bromley Ct. ST1	31 E4
Bromley Hough. ST4	46 C2
Bromley St. ST1	31 E4
Brompton Dri. ST2	27 E3
Bromsberrow Way. ST3	56 C4
Bromsgrove Pl. ST3	48 D5
Bronte Gro. ST2	26 C4
Brook Clo, Blythe Bridge. ST11	60 E2
Brook Clo, Endon. ST9	20 C1
Brook Cotts. ST9	20 C1
Brook Gate. ST11	60 E1
Brook La, Endon. ST9	20 C1
Brook La, Newcastle. ST5	39 G5
Brook Pl. ST4	40 C2
Brook Rd. ST4	53 E4
Brook St, Silverdale. ST5	37 H2
Brook St, Stoke. ST4	41 F5
Brooke Pl. ST5	45 H2
Brookes Ct. ST4	42 B6
Brookfield Av. ST9	20 B3
Brookfield Ct. ST1	6 B1
Brookfield Rd, Baddeley Edge. ST2	27 F2
Brookfield Rd, Trent Vale. ST4	46 B3
Brookhouse Dri. ST12	59 E4
Brookhouse La. ST2	33 G6
Brookhouse Rd, Crackley. ST5	22 D5
Brookhouse Rd, Weston Coyney. ST3	50 C5
Brookland Rd. ST6	16 C5
Brooklands Av. ST3	54 D1
Brooklawns Dri. ST3	43 E6
Brookmead Gro. ST3	43 E6
Brookside Clo. ST5	39 E5
Brookside Dri, Endon. ST9	20 C1
Brookside Dri, Hollybush. ST3	48 A5

Brookview Dri. ST3	50 B4
Brookwood Clo. ST5	45 F5
Brookwood Dri. ST5	50 C5
Broom St. ST1	6 C1
Broome Hill. ST5	44 B5
Broomfield Pl Nth. ST1	31 E6
Broomfield Pl Sth. ST1	31 E6
Broomfield Rd. ST6	18 A5
Broomhill St. ST6	23 H1
Brough La. ST4	53 F4
Broughton Cres. ST12	59 G5
Broughton Rd, Basford. ST2	40 A2
Broughton Rd, Bucknall. ST2	42 C1
Brown St. ST6	25 E6
Brownfield Rd. ST3	50 C6
Brownhill Rd, Brown Edge. ST6	18 D2
Brownhills Rd, Tunstall. ST6	24 B3
Browning Rd. ST3	48 B6
Brownley Rd. ST6	25 H5
Brownsea Pl. ST3	48 A3
Brundall Oval. ST2	43 G2
Brunswick Pl. ST1	6 C6
Brunswick St, Hanley. ST1	6 B4
Brunswick St, Newcastle. ST5	39 G3
Brunt St. ST6	30 A1
Brutus Rd. ST5	28 B3
Bryan St. ST1	6 B1
Bryant Pl. ST2	33 E5
Bryant Rd. ST2	33 E4
Brymbo Rd. ST5	28 D4
Buccleuch Rd. ST3	49 G6
Buckingham Cres. ST4	52 D1
Buckland Gro. ST4	59 E1
Buckley Rd. ST6	17 F5
Buckleys Row. ST5	39 F4
Buckmaster Av. ST5	45 H1
Bucknall New Rd. ST1	6 D3
Bucknall Old Rd. ST1	31 H5
Bucknall Rd. ST1	32 B6
Bull La. ST7	16 A1
Buller St. ST1	41 H2
Bulstrode St. ST6	24 B6
Bunny Hill. ST6	45 H2
Bunts La. ST9	27 F1
Burford Av. ST5	22 B4
Burford Way. ST2	42 D2
Burgess St. ST6	30 B1
Burgundy Gro. ST3	56 C3
Burland Rd. ST5	22 A4
Burleigh Gro. ST5	30 A6
Burlidge Rd. ST6	16 D4
Burlington Av. ST6	30 B6
Burmarsh Walk. ST6	30 D1
Burnett Pl. ST6	26 A1
Burnham St. ST4	48 D2
Burnhays Rd. ST6	24 C4
Burnley St. ST1	31 H3
Burns Row. ST3	50 D5
Burnside Clo. ST3	56 C3
Burnwood Pl. ST6	17 E5
Burrington Dri. ST4	53 F6
Burslem Greenway. ST6	25 E6
Bursley Way. ST5	23 E6
Burt St. ST3	50 D5
Burton Cres. ST1	32 A2
Burton Pl. ST1	6 C3
Bute St. ST4	48 D3
Butler St. ST4	41 F6
Butterfield Pl. ST6	24 B2
Buttermere Clo. ST6	24 B5
Butts Grn. ST2	33 F2
Buxton Av. ST5	37 F2
Buxton St. ST1	31 H1
Byatts Gro. ST3	48 D5
Bycars La. ST6	24 D4
Bycars Rd. ST6	24 D5
Bylands Pl. ST5	45 F3
Byron St. ST4	40 A3
Bywater Gro. ST3	49 G1
Cadeby Gro. ST2	26 D4
Cadman Cres. ST6	26 A2
Cairn Clo. ST2	33 G6
Caistor Clo. ST2	26 D4
Caldbeck Pl. ST1	31 H5

Caldew Gro. ST4	53 G6
Caledonia Rd. ST4	41 E2
California St. ST3	48 D4
Callender Pl. ST6	25 E5
Calrofold Dri. ST5	22 B4
Calvary Cres. ST2	43 G4
Calver St. ST6	24 A2
Calverley St. ST3	49 G5
Calvert Gro. ST5	29 F2
Camberwell Gro. ST4	53 G5
Camborne Cres. ST5	45 E2
Cambrian Way. ST2	33 E5
Cambridge Ct. ST5	46 A3
Cambridge Dri. ST5	46 A3
Cambridge St. ST1	6 A5
Camden St. ST4	48 B3
Camellia Clo. ST4	40 B3
Camelot Clo. ST4	58 D1
Camillus Rd. ST5	38 C2
Camoys Rd. ST6	30 D1
Camp Rd. ST6	25 G4
Campbell Rd. ST4	47 E3
Campbell Ter. ST1	32 A3
Campion Av. ST5	40 A1
Canal La. ST6	24 A4
Canal Side. ST6	59 F5
Canary Rd. ST2	24 A6
Canberra Cres. ST3	43 G5
Canning St. ST4	57 E4
Cannon Pl. ST1	48 B2
Cannon St. ST1	6 A6
Canterbury Dri. ST6	6 B6
Canvey Gro. ST3	25 F1
Cape St. ST1	56 D4
Capesthorne Clo. ST9	6 B1
Capewell St. ST3	34 D6
Capper St. ST7	49 F3
Capricorn Way. ST6	24 B2
Caraway Pl. ST3	16 C4
Carberry Way. ST3	56 C5
Card St. ST6	50 B3
Cardiff Gro. ST1	30 D1
Cardigan Gro. ST4	6 B6
Cardington Clo. ST5	53 G4
Cardway. ST5	45 E4
Cardwell St. ST1	23 F6
Carina Gdns. ST6	32 A4
Carisbrooke Way. ST4	25 H5
Carling Gro. ST4	53 G6
Carlisle St. ST3	48 D2
Carlos Pl. ST5	55 E1
Carlton Av, Brown Edge. ST6	23 F5
Carlton Av, Tunstall. ST6	19 E4
Carlton Av, Westbury Park. ST5	24 D1
Carlton Clo. ST6	45 G4
Carlton Rd. ST4	19 E4
Carlton Pl. ST1	41 G4
Carmount Rd. ST2	25 H6
Carnation Clo. ST3	33 E1
Carnforth Gro. ST6	50 D1
Caroline Clo. ST9	16 C2
Caroline Cres. ST6	34 D4
Caroline St. ST3	19 E4
Carpenter Rd. ST3	49 E4
Carr St, ST7	48 D4
Carroll Pl. ST4	16 A1
Carroll Dri. ST3	52 D1
Carron St. ST4	49 G3
Carryer Pl. ST5	49 E2
Carson St. ST6	38 D4
Cartlidge St. ST4	24 D3
Cartmel Pl. ST6	40 A3
Casewell Rd. ST6	25 E2
Caspian Gro. ST4	31 G1
Castel Clo. ST5	53 F3
Castle Gro. ST2	44 C4
Castle Hill Rd. ST5	33 E4
*Castle Keep Mews, Silverdale Rd. ST5	39 F3
Castle Mount. ST5	38 C2
Castle Ridge. ST5	28 C2
Castle St, Chesterton. ST5	39 E4
Castle St, Newcastle. ST5	28 C1
Castledine Gro. ST3	39 H3
Castlefield St. ST4	49 G3
	41 E2

66

Street	Ref
Coronation Rd, Newcastle. ST5	39 H4
Coronation St. ST6	24 B1
Corporation St, Newcastle. ST5	39 G3
Corporation St, Stoke. ST4	47 E1
Coseley St. ST6	25 G4
Cotehill Rd. ST9	34 D4
Cotesheath St. ST1	41 H3
Coton Rise. ST12	59 F5
Cotswold Av. ST5	28 C6
Cotswold Cres. ST2	26 C5
Cottage Clo. ST3	56 A2
Cotterill Dri. ST5	23 G5
Cotterill Gro. ST6	30 D1
Cottons Row. ST4	40 A4
Cottonwood Gro. ST3	49 F3
Coupe Dri. ST3	50 C2
Court La. ST6	29 G4
Court No. 1. ST3	49 H6
Courtney Pl. ST3	56 A2
Courtway Dri. ST1	25 H6
Coverdale Clo. ST3	56 C3
Coverley Rd. ST1	46 D1
Cowen St. ST6	18 A4
Cowley Way. ST2	43 H5
Cowlishaw Rd. ST6	17 F4
Cowper St. ST4	48 C1
Coyney Gro. ST3	50 C4
Crabtree Clo. ST4	42 B4
Crackley Bank. ST5	22 C3
Cranberry Dri. ST5	22 B4
Cranbourne Av. ST2	26 D3
Cranbrook Clo. ST4	52 D3
Crane St. ST1	31 F3
Cranfield Pl. ST2	42 E2
Cranford Way. ST2	33 G6
Cranleigh Av. ST1	25 H6
Cranmer St. ST4	41 F5
Cranswick Gro. ST2	43 H3
Cranwell Pl. ST3	56 A2
Cranwood Rd. ST12	58 B5
Cranworth Gro. ST3	55 H2
Craven Clo. ST4	53 E3
Crawford St. ST4	47 H2
Crediton Av. ST6	25 F1
Crep La. ST6	31 F2
Crescent Gro. ST4	40 B3
Cresswell Av. ST5	22 B5
Cresswell Rd. ST1	32 A6
Crestbrook Rd. ST2	33 E2
Crestfield Rd. ST3	56 A2
Crestway Rd. ST2	27 F3
Crick Rd. ST1	42 A2
Critchlow Gro. ST3	54 C1
Croft Av. ST5	29 F3
Croft Clo. ST6	25 G4
Croft Cres. ST4	46 D1
Croft Rd. ST5	39 G2
Croft St. ST6	24 C6
Crofters Ct. ST5	22 B2
Croftfield St. ST2	43 G4
Cromartie St. ST3	49 F6
Cromer Cres. ST1	32 A4
Cromer Rd. ST1	32 A5
Cromer St. ST5	30 A5
Crompton Gro. ST4	53 G6
Cromwell St. ST1	31 H2
Crosby Rd. ST4	46 B4
Cross Edge. ST6	19 E3
Cross May St. ST5	39 F4
Cross St, Chesterton. ST5	22 B6
Cross St, Longbridge Hayes. ST6	23 H6
Cross St, ·Weston Coyney. ST3	50 D2
Crossdale Av. ST2	26 D3
Crossfield Av. ST11	60 D3
Crossland Pl East. ST3	56 C2
Crossland Pl West. ST3	56 B2
Crossley Rd. ST6	24 D3
Crossmead Gro. ST1	32 C3
Crossway Rd. ST6	31 G1
Croston St. ST1	41 F2
Crouch Av. ST6	24 D1
Crowcrofts Rd. ST4	54 A4
Crown St, Hanley. ST1	6 A5
Crown St, Silverdale. ST5	37 H2
Crowndale Pl. ST6	16 B2
Crowther St. ST4	41 F4
Croxden Rd. ST2	33 E3
Croyde Pl. ST3	56 C5
Crystal St. ST6	31 F2
Cumberbatch Av. ST6	17 E3
Cumberland St, Fenton. ST4	42 B6
Cumberland St, Newcastle. ST5	39 H3
Cumming St. ST4	40 B3
Curland St. ST3	50 A5
Curlew Rd. ST6	16 C1
Curtis Pl. ST3	56 D5
Curzon Rd. ST6	25 E3
Curzon St. ST5	40 A1
Cutts St. ST1	41 F2
Cynthia Gro. ST6	25 E3
Cypress Gro, Blythe Bridge. ST11	60 E3
Cypress Gro, Crackley. ST5	22 B6
Dace Gro. ST6	25 F2
Dahlia Clo. ST3	50 D1
Dain Pl. ST5	29 G2
Dain St. ST6	24 G6
Daintry St. ST4	46 D3
Dairyfields Way. ST1	25 G6
Daisy Pl. ST4	48 B3
Dale Av. ST6	18 A4
Dale St. ST6	24 B6
Dale View. ST3	50 D4
Dalecot Grn. ST2	43 G4
Dalegarth Gro. ST3	56 A2
Dalehall Gdns. ST6	24 B6
Dalehead Ct. ST3	56 B2
Daleian Ct. ST5	38 A2
Daleview Dri. ST5	37 H3
Dalewood Rd. ST5	28 C4
Dalton Gro. ST2	43 G3
Daly Cres. ST5	37 G2
Dane Hill Gro. ST4	52 C1
Dane Walk. ST1	31 H5
Danebower Rd. ST4	53 F5
Danebridge Gro. ST1	32 B3
Danemead Clo. ST3	56 C3
Danescroft . ST4	53 E4
Darius Clo. ST5	23 G6
Darnley St. ST4	41 G4
Darrall Gdns. ST4	46 B4
Darsham Gdns. ST5	45 G6
Dart Av. ST6	24 D1
Dart Pl. ST5	45 E4
Dartford Pl. ST6	25 F1
Dartmouth Av. ST5	45 E1
Dartmouth Pl. ST3	56 A2
Dartmouth St. ST6	24 E5
Dash Gro. ST6	25 G5
Davenport St. ST6	24 A6
Davenport Way. ST5	44 D4
Daventry Clo. ST2	42 C2
David Rd. ST3	56 A1
Davis St. ST4	41 E2
Davison St. ST6	31 E1
Davy Clo. ST2	42 D1
Dawlish Dri. ST2	43 E1
Dawn Av. ST6	25 E1
Dayson Pl. ST5	29 F1
Deakin Gro. ST5	45 H1
Deakin Rd. ST6	17 E5
Dean Pl. ST1	42 A2
Dean St. ST2	33 F5
Deans La. ST5	22 A4
Deansberry Clo. ST4	52 D2
Deanscroft Way. ST3	49 H3
Deansgate. ST5	39 E4
Deansway. ST4	53 E4
Deaville Rd. ST2	33 E6
Debenham Cres. ST2	42 C2
Decade Clo. ST5	22 D3
Dee La. ST5	45 F4
Deepdale Clo. ST6	26 B4
Defoe St. ST3	50 A3
Delamere Gro. ST5	39 G2
Delamere Gro. ST4	52 D4
Delaney Dri. ST3	50 B3
Delius Gro. ST1	32 C3
Dellwood Gro. ST3	49 G1
Delph Walk. ST4	48 C1
Delves Pl. ST5	45 F2
Denbigh Clo. ST5	45 H4
Denbigh St. ST1	31 E4
Denby Av. ST3	49 E2
Dency Gro. ST6	25 E2
Dene Side. ST5	39 E4
Denewell Clo. ST3	50 C6
Denewood Pl. ST3	56 D1
Denham Sq. ST3	54 B2
Dennington Cres. ST3	54 B2
Dennis St. ST4	48 C1
Dennis Viollet Av. ST4	47 G4
Denry Cres. ST5	29 F1
Denstone Cres. ST3	48 C6
Dentdale Clo. ST3	56 B3
Denton Clo. ST5	45 G4
Denton Gro. ST3	50 A4
Derby Pl. ST5	45 H3
Derby St. ST1	6 D5
Dereham Way. ST2	43 H2
Derek Dri. ST1	32 A2
Derry St. ST4	48 A3
Derwent Pl. ST5	29 F6
Derwent St. ST1	31 E3
Devane Walk. ST3	51 E6
Devon Clo. ST5	45 G3
Devon Way. ST3	55 G2
Devonshire Sq. ST2	43 F3
Dewsbury Rd. ST4	42 A5
Diamond Clo, Barlaston. ST12	59 E6
Diamond Clo, Meir Heath. ST5	55 G5
Diamond Ridge. ST12	59 E6
Diana Rd. ST1	32 B2
Diarmid Rd. ST4	46 C6
Dickens St. ST2	33 F5
Dickenson Rd East. ST6	31 G1
Dickenson Rd West. ST6	31 G1
Dilhorne Gro. ST3	55 F1
Dilhorne La. ST11	51 H5
Dilhorne Rd. ST11	60 F2
Dilke St. ST1	31 H4
Dill Gro. ST3	56 C5
Dimmelow St. ST3	50 D2
Dimsdale Parade East. ST5	29 G3
Dimsdale Parade West. ST5	29 E2
Dimsdale St. ST6	30 C2
Dimsdale View. ST3	28 D2
Dimsdale View E. ST5	29 F2
Dimsdale View W. ST5	29 F2
Dividy Rd. ST2	42 C1
Dixons Row. ST5	28 B1
Dobell Gro. ST3	49 G3
Dobson St. ST6	31 F1
Doddington Pl. ST5	45 F1
Dogcroft Rd. ST6	17 F6
Dolespring Clo. ST11	60 E1
Dollys La. ST6	24 D3
Dominic St. ST4	40 D4
Donald Rd. ST1	32 A2
Doncaster La. ST4	40 D6
Dorcas Dri. ST3	48 B3
Dorchester Walk. ST2	43 F1
Dorian Way. ST9	20 C2
Dorking Clo. ST2	42 C2
Dorlan Clo. ST9	27 F2
Dorridge Gro. ST5	30 B5
Dorrington Clo. ST2	26 D4
Dorrington Gro. ST5	29 H2
Dorset Clo. ST2	33 F6
Dorset Pl. ST5	46 A3
Douglas Av. ST4	46 C2
Douglas Pl. ST1	42 A2
Douglas Rd. ST5	39 E1
Douglas St. ST1	31 F3
Doulton Dri. ST5	29 G1
Doulton St. ST6	24 D5
Dove Pl. ST5	45 F4
Dove Rd. ST11	60 E2
Dovebank Gro. ST5	55 C5
Dovecote Clo. ST3	56 A2
Dovedale Pl. ST5	37 G3
Dover Pl. ST1	31 H4
Doveridge St. ST4	47 G2
Down View. ST3	50 D4
Downey St. ST1	6 C6
Downfield Pl. ST2	26 C4
Downham Rd. ST5	38 C1
Downing Av. ST5	30 B6
Downsview Gro. ST3	48 B5
Dragon Sq. ST5	22 C6
Drake Clo. ST2	42 C3
Drakeford Ct. ST6	18 A6
Drakeford Gro. ST6	18 A6
Draw-Well Lane. ST9	34 D4
Draycott Dri. ST5	22 A4
Draycott Old Rd. ST11	60 E2
Drayton Gdns. ST2	42 C2
Drayton Rd. ST3	49 E3
Drayton St. ST5	39 F4
Dresden St. ST1	31 H6
Driffield Clo. ST2	43 H3
Droitwich Clo. ST5	37 E1
Drubbery La. ST3	48 C6
Drumburn Clo. ST6	16 C3
Dryberg Way. ST2	32 D5
Dryden Rd. ST6	30 D2
Duddell Rd. ST6	25 G4
Dudley Pl. ST3	56 B2
Duesbury Grn. ST3	48 D4
Duke Bank Ter. ST6	18 B6
Duke Pl. ST5	38 A3
Duke St, Heron Cross. ST4	48 B3
Duke St, Newcastle. ST5	39 H5
Dulverton Av. ST5	45 E2
Duncalf Gro. ST5	29 G1
Duncalf St. ST6	24 C6
Duncan St. ST4	42 A6
Dundas St. ST1	31 H4
Dundee Rd. ST3	48 D6
Dundee St. ST3	39 F3
Dunkirk. ST7	39 F3
Dunkirk Ct. ST7	39 F3
Dunning St. ST6	24 A1
Dunrobin St. ST3	49 F6
Dunsany Gro. ST1	32 A2
Dunsford Av. ST2	26 D4
Dunster Rd. ST3	49 E2
Dunwood Dri. ST5	25 E2
Durber Clo. ST4	46 B3
Durham Dri. ST3	55 F3
Durham Gro. ST5	46 A3
Durston Pl. ST3	50 A5
Dyke St. ST1	6 D2
Dylan Rd. ST3	49 G4
Eagle St. ST1	32 A5
Eamont Av. ST6	25 E1
Eardley St. ST4	40 D6
Earl St, Newcastle. ST5	39 H3
Earl St, Silverdale. ST5	37 H3
Earls Ct. ST5	39 H3
Earls Dri. ST5	45 G1
Earls Rd. ST4	53 F4
Earlsbrook Dri. ST4	53 F3
Earlswood Dri. ST1	32 C3
Easdale Pl. ST5	45 G2
Easedale Clo. ST2	26 D4
East Bank Ride. ST11	60 E1
East Cres. ST5	40 A1
East Gro. ST3	48 D5
East St. ST3	50 D2
East Ter. ST6	17 F4
East View. ST6	30 C1
Eastbank Rd. ST1	31 E4
Eastbourne Rd. ST1	32 A5
Eastbridge Av. ST1	25 H6
Eastdean Av. ST2	42 C2
Easters Gro. ST2	27 E5
Easthead Walk. ST1	41 E1
Eastwick Cres. ST4	52 D2
Eastwood Av. ST6	25 E1
Eastwood Pl. ST1	6 C6
Eastwood Rd. ST1	6 D5
Eaton St. ST1	31 H5
Eaves La. ST2	33 F4
Eaveswood Rd. ST2	33 F3
Ebury Gro. ST3	56 A1
Ecclestone Pl. ST6	17 E4
Edale Clo. ST5	37 G3
Eddisbury Dri. ST5	22 B3
Eden Gro. ST3	56 B1
Edenhurst Av. ST3	56 D2
Edensor Rd. ST3	49 E5
Edensor St. ST5	22 C6
Edensor Ter. ST3	48 D5
Edgar Pl. ST3	49 F1
Edgbaston Dri. ST4	53 H3

Heather Clo. ST9	34 C4
Heather Cres. ST3	55 G5
Heather Hills. ST9	19 G5
Heather View. ST6	18 A4
Heatherlands Clo. ST3	55 F5
Heatherleigh Gro. ST1	32 B3
Heathfield Dri. ST5	22 B4
Heathfield Gro. ST5	56 B5
Heathfield Rd. ST6	17 G6
Heaton Ter. ST5	29 G2
Heber St. ST3	49 F3
Hedley Pl. ST5	39 E4
Helston Av. ST3	49 H4
Heming Pl. ST2	32 C6
Hemingway Rd. ST3	49 G3
Hemlock Rd. ST3	49 F3
Hempstalls Gro. ST5	29 G6
Hempstalls La. ST5	39 G2
Henderson Gro. ST3	50 D5
Henley Clo. ST12	59 G1
Henry St. ST6	24 A1
Henshall Rd. ST5	22 D6
Herbert Rd. ST3	49 G5
Herbert St. ST4	41 H6
Herd St. ST6	24 C4
Hereford Av. ST5	45 G3
Hereford Gro. ST2	43 G2
Herm Clo. ST5	44 C3
Hermes Clo. ST3	57 E4
Heron St. ST4	48 A2
Hertford Gro. ST5	45 H4
Hertford St. ST4	48 B3
Hesketh Av. ST6	18 A5
Heskin Way. ST6	17 E4
Hester Clo. ST3	43 F6
Hethersett Walk. ST2	43 G2
Hewitt Cres. ST9	34 C5
Hewitt St. ST6	16 D4
Heyburn Cres. ST6	24 B5
Heysham Clo. ST3	50 D3
Hickman St. ST5	39 F3
Hide St. ST4	41 E6
High Bank Pl. ST6	25 F4
High La, Brown Edge. ST6	18 D5
High La, Great Chell. ST6	16 D4
High St, Caverswall. ST11	51 G5
High St, Chesterton. ST5	28 C1
High St, Knutton. ST5	38 C1
High St, May Bank. ST5	29 H6
High St, Newcastle. ST5	39 G3
High St, Sandyford. ST6	16 A6
High St, Silverdale. ST5	37 F2
High St, Tunstall. ST6	24 B2
High St, Wolstanton. ST5	29 H2
High View. ST3	55 F5
High View Rd. ST9	20 B1
Highbury Rd. ST9	35 E4
Highcroft Walk. ST6	25 F4
Higherland. ST5	39 E4
Highfield Av, Meir. ST3	56 A1
Highfield Av, Wolstanton. ST5	30 A5
Highfield Clo. ST11	57 F4
Highfield Ct. ST5	45 G1
Highfield Dri. ST3	48 A4
Highfield Grange. ST5	30 B6
Highfields Rise. ST4	52 C3
Highgate Clo. ST6	26 B2
Highgrove Rd. ST4	46 C4
Highland Av. ST11	57 H4
Highland Dri. ST3	55 G2
Highton St. ST2	27 E5
Highville Pl. ST4	46 D2
Highway La. ST5	36 B6
Higson Av. ST4	41 E5
Hilderstone Rd. ST3	55 F5
Hill St, Newcastle. ST5	39 F2
Hill St, Stoke. ST4	41 E5
Hill Top Cres. ST3	55 F5
Hill View. ST2	27 E3
Hill Village Rd. ST9	35 E4
Hillary St. ST6	31 F2
Hillberry Clo. ST2	42 D2
Hillchurch St. ST1	6 C2
Hillcrest St. ST1	6 D3
Hillfield Av. ST4	46 B3

Hillgreen Rd. ST3	49 G1
Hillman St. ST2	27 E5
Hillport Av. ST5	29 F1
Hillside. ST5	39 E5
Hillside Av, Endon. ST9	20 B2
Hillside Av, Forsbrook. ST11	60 E2
Hillside Av, Meir. ST3	56 A1
Hillside Clo. ST2	27 F3
Hillside Rd, Baddeley Edge. ST2	27 F3
Hillside Rd, Werrington. ST9	34 C4
Hillside Walk. ST4	40 A4
Hillswood Clo. ST9	20 B2
Hillswood Dri. ST9	20 B2
Hilltop Av. ST5	40 B1
Hilltop Clo. ST6	19 E1
Hilton Rd. ST4	40 B6
Hincho Pl. ST6	18 A6
Hinckley Gro. ST4	53 F6
Hinde St. ST1	6 B6
Hines St. ST4	48 A2
Hinton Clo. ST3	54 C2
Hitchman St	48 A1
Hobart St. ST6	31 E1
Hobby Clo. ST3	56 C4
Hobson St. ST6	25 E6
Hodgkinson St. ST5	28 D2
Hodnet Gro. ST1	31 F3
Hogarth Pl. ST5	28 C2
Holbeach Av. ST2	42 C2
Holborn. ST5	39 F3
Holbrook Walk. ST2	43 E2
Holdcroft Rd. ST2	33 E4
Holden Av. ST5	30 A6
Holden Av Nth. ST6	25 H6
Holden Av Sth. ST6	25 H6
Holder St. ST1	31 F3
Holditch Rd. ST5	28 D4
Holehouse Rd. ST2	33 E3
Holland St. ST6	24 A1
Hollies Dri. ST3	55 F5
Hollings St. ST4	48 D2
Hollington Dri. ST6	17 E2
Hollinshead Av. ST5	29 F5
Hollowood Pl. ST6	18 A6
Hollowood Walk. ST6	18 A6
Holly Ct. ST2	43 H5
Holly Dri. ST2	34 C5
Holly Pl. ST4	48 B3
Holly Rd. ST5	22 B5
Hollybank. ST4	52 C4
Hollybank Cres. ST4	46 D3
Hollybush Cres. ST3	48 A4
Hollybush Rd. ST3	48 A4
Hollywood La. ST5	36 B3
Holm Clo. ST4	47 E3
Holmes Way. ST6	17 F2
Holmesfield Walk. ST3	49 G4
Holst Dri. ST1	32 C3
Holyhead Cres. ST3	50 D3
Homer Pl. ST6	17 F5
Homer St. ST1	32 A6
Homestead St. ST1	43 H4
Honeysuckle Av. ST11	60 D4
Honeywall. ST4	40 D6
Honeywood. ST5	39 G1
Honiton Walk. ST3	49 G4
Hoon Av. ST5	29 G5
Hoover St. ST6	24 A2
Hope St. ST1	6 B1
Hopedale Clo, Sandford Hill. ST4	43 E6
Hopedale Clo, Westbury Park. ST5	45 G5
Hopton Way. ST6	17 E2
Hopwood Pl. ST2	33 E6
Horatius Rd. ST5	28 B3
Hordley St. ST1	6 D4
Hornby Row. ST4	41 E6
Horsley Gro. ST3	54 A2
Horton Dri. ST3	50 C2
Horton St. ST5	40 A3
Horwood Gdns. ST6	25 G5
Hose St. ST6	24 A2
Hoskins Rd. ST6	16 B6
Hot La. ST6	25 E6
Hough Hill. ST6	19 E1
Houghton St. ST1	41 G1
Houghwood La. ST9	27 H1

Houldsworth Dri. ST6	17 E3
Housefield Rd. ST2	43 G4
Houseman Dri. ST3	50 A3
Houston Av. ST9	20 B1
Hoveringham Dri. ST2	42 B2
Howard Clo. ST9	34 C4
Howard Gro. ST5	39 E6
Howard Pl, Hanley. ST1	41 F2
Howard Pl, Newcastle. ST5	39 E6
Howard St. ST3	49 E6
Howe Gro. ST5	38 C2
Howson St. ST1	6 D6
Hudson Walk. ST3	49 F4
Hughes Av. ST5	39 F1
Hughes St. ST6	31 E1
Hulland Clo. ST5	37 G3
Hulme Clo. ST6	17 H3
Hulme La. ST9	34 C6
Hulme Rd. ST3	50 A2
Hulme St. ST4	40 C4
Hulse St. ST4	48 D1
Hulton Rd. ST2	33 E3
Hulton St. ST1	31 H4
Humber St. ST1	40 D1
Humber Way. ST5	45 F4
Hunt St. ST6	24 B2
Huntbach St. ST1	6 C3
Hunters Dri. ST4	46 D1
Hunters Way. ST4	46 D1
Huntilee Rd. ST6	24 C2
Huntingdon Pl. ST1	32 C2
Huntley Av. ST4	46 D1
Huntsbank Dri. ST5	22 B4
Huron Gro. ST4	53 E3
Hurst St. ST3	48 D4
Hutchinson Walk. ST5	48 C5
Hutton Way. ST2	43 G2
Huxley Pl. ST3	49 G4
Hyacinth Ct. ST5	39 G1
Hyacinth Rd. ST4	40 B2
Hyndley Clo. ST2	42 D1
Ibsen Rd. ST3	50 B3
Ilam Clo. ST5	37 G3
Ilford Side. ST3	54 B2
Ilkley Pl. ST5	37 E2
Imandra Clo. ST4	53 E3
Imogen Clo. ST4	49 E1
Imperial Ct. ST1	41 H2
INDUSTRIAL & RETAIL:	
Brampton Ind Est. ST5	39 F2
Britannia Park Ind Est. ST6	31 F1
Cinderhill Ind Est. ST3	50 A4
Etruria Trading Est. ST4	40 B1
Far Green Ind Est. ST1	31 H3
Fen Park Ind Est. ST4	48 C2
Fenton Ind Est. ST4	42 B4
Hamilton Ind Est. ST4	48 A1
High Carr Business Pk. ST5	22 D3
Holditch Ind Est. ST5	29 E4
Hot La Ind Est. ST6	25 E6
Hyde Park Ind Est. ST4	41 G6
Imex Business Pk. ST4	48 B2
Longbridge Hayes Ind Est. ST6	23 F4
Longport Enterprise Centre. ST6	24 A6
Loomer Rd Ind Est. ST5	28 C3
Loomers Rd Ind Est. ST5	28 C4
Lymedale Pk Ind Est. ST	28 C4
Marcus Ind Est. ST2	32 B6
New Forest Ind Est. ST1	31 G4
Newcastle Business Centre. ST5	23 E5
Newstead Trading Est. ST4	53 H4
Norton Ind Est. ST6	26 A3
Oldfield Ind Est. ST4	48 C2
Parkhouse Ind Est East. ST5	23 E4
Parkhouse Ind Est West. ST5	22 D6
Ravenside Retail Pk. ST4	41 H4
Rowhurst Clo. Ind Est. ST5	28 A2
Scotia Business Pk. ST6	24 B3
Scott Lidgett Ind Est. ST6	30 A1

Sneyd Ind Est. ST6	25 F5
Springfields Retail Pk. ST4	46 B2
Stoke Business Pk. ST4	41 F6
Stoke-on-Trent Enterprise Pk. ST1	41 E2
Stonewall Ind Est. ST5	38 B2
Wolstanton Retail Park. ST5	30 B5
Worldgate Centre. ST4	53 H3
Ingelow Clo. ST3	48 D6
Ingestre Sq. ST3	54 B2
Ingleborough Pl. ST2	27 G5
Inglefield Av. ST6	25 F4
Ingleton Gro. ST3	56 C3
Inglewood Dri. ST5	29 H2
Inglewood Gro. ST5	29 H2
Inglis St. ST4	41 G5
Intake Rd. ST5	18 A6
Iona Pl. ST3	48 C5
Ipswich Walk. ST2	43 E1
Irene Av, Basford. ST5	40 A1
Irene Av, Tunstall. ST6	24 D2
Iris Clo. ST3	51 E2
Ironbridge Dri. ST5	38 D2
Ironmarket. ST5	39 G3
Irvine Rd. ST9	35 E4
Islay Walk. ST3	48 C5
Ivy Clo. ST11	60 D3
Ivy Gro. ST4	52 C2
Ivy House Rd. ST1	32 A6
Ivyhouse Dri. ST12	59 G1
Jack Ashley Ct. ST4	48 A1
Jack Haye La. ST3	27 G5
Jackfield St. ST6	25 E4
Jackson St. ST6	24 D5
Jacqueline St. ST6	23 H1
Jade Ct. ST3	49 G3
Jamage Rd. ST7	22 B1
James Brindley Clo. ST1	41 E1
James Cres. ST9	35 E4
James St, Boothen. ST4	46 C2
James St, Dimsdale. ST5	29 H3
Janet Pl. ST1	32 A4
Janson St. ST4	52 C1
Jasmine Clo. ST11	60 D3
Jasmine Way. ST7	16 A1
Jason St. ST5	39 F2
Jasper Clo, Barlaston Park. ST12	59 H1
Jasper Clo, Porthill. ST5	29 G2
Jasper St. ST1	6 C6
Java Cres. ST4	53 F3
Jaycean Av. ST6	16 B6
Jean Clo. ST6	24 D3
Jefferson St. ST6	24 A1
Jenkins St. ST6	24 D5
Jenkinson Clo. ST5	39 E5
Jerbourg Clo. ST5	44 C4
Jeremy Clo. ST4	46 D1
Jersey Clo. ST5	44 C3
Jersey Cres. ST3	55 F2
Jervis St. ST1	31 H4
Jervison St. ST3	49 G1
Jesmond Gro. ST3	54 A3
Joanhurst Cres. ST1	41 E1
John Bright St. ST1	31 H4
John O'Gaunts Rd. ST5	39 F3
John Rhodes Way. ST6	16 A5
John St, Crackley. ST5	22 C6
John St, Hanley. ST1	6 B5
John St, Knutton. ST5	38 D1
John St, Newcastle. ST5	40 A3
Johnson Av. ST5	29 E5
Johnson Pl. ST6	17 E4
Johnson St. ST5	28 B1
Johnstone Av. ST9	35 E4
Jolley St. ST6	25 G4
Jolyon Clo. ST4	49 E1
Jonathan Rd. ST4	53 G6
Jordan St. ST1	41 E1
Joseph St. ST6	24 C6
Josiah Wedgwood St. ST1	31 E6
Joyce Av. ST6	25 F3
Jubilee Rd. ST1	41 E1
Jubilee Rd, Trentham. ST4	52 C2
Jubilee Rd, Wolstanton. ST5	30 A6
Judith Gro. ST4	47 G3

Street	Ref
June Rd. ST4	49 E1
Juniper Clo, Meir Park. ST3	56 C5
Juniper Clo, Waterhayes Village. ST5	22 C4
Jupiter St. ST6	25 G4
Justin Clo. ST5	30 A2
Kara Pl. ST4	53 F3
*Kartley St, Quinton Walk. ST6	25 G3
Kaydor Clo. ST9	34 D4
Kearsley Way. ST3	54 A2
Keary St. ST4	47 E1
Keble Way. ST3	48 C6
Kedleston Rd. ST6	25 E4
Keele By-Pass. ST5	36 C4
Keele Rd. CW3	36 A4
Keele Rd, Keele. ST5	37 E6
Keele St. ST6	24 A1
Keeling St. ST5	29 H3
Keelings Dri. ST4	46 B3
Keelings Rd, Hanley. ST1	31 H4
Keelings Rd, Northwood. ST6	32 A5
Keene Clo. ST6	26 B2
Keepers Clo. ST11	60 E3
Kelly Grn. ST6	17 E4
Kelman Rd. ST4	42 D6
Kelmore Clo. ST3	49 E3
Kelsall St. ST6	25 E4
Kelvin Av. ST1	31 H2
Kelvin St. ST5	30 A5
Kemball St. ST4	47 G3
Kemnay Av. ST6	17 E2
Kempthorne Rd. ST1	42 A2
Kendal Gro. ST2	43 G2
Kendal Pl. ST5	45 G1
Kendrick St. ST3	49 G4
Kenelyn Cres. ST3	48 A4
Kenilworth Gro, Basford. ST5	30 B6
Kenilworth Gro, Meir. ST3	56 B1
Kenley Av. ST9	20 B1
Kennedy Rd. ST4	53 E4
Kennedy Walk. ST9	34 D4
Kennermont Rd. ST2	33 F3
Kennet Clo. ST5	45 F4
Kennington Oval. ST4	53 G3
Kensington Ct. ST4	46 C4
Kensington Rd. ST4	46 D4
Kensworth Clo. ST5	45 E4
Kent Clo. ST4	42 A6
Kent Dri. ST9	20 B3
Kent Gro. ST5	22 B6
Kent Pl. ST4	42 A6
Kentmere Clo. ST4	49 E2
Kentmere Pl. ST5	45 G1
Kents Row. ST12	59 G4
Kenworthy St. ST6	24 B1
Kervis Gro. ST3	56 D4
Kestrel Av. ST3	57 E4
Keswick Pl. ST5	45 G1
Kettering Dri. ST2	42 B2
Ketton Clo. ST6	17 E1
Keynsham Walk. ST6	25 G3
Keyworth Walk. ST2	42 C2
Kibworth Gro. ST1	31 G3
Kidbrooke Pl. ST3	54 A2
Kilburn Pl. ST2	42 C2
Kildare St. ST3	49 F6
Kildnown Clo. ST1	41 E1
Kilsby Gro. ST2	27 E4
Kimberley Grange. ST5	39 G1
Kimberley Rd, Hanley. ST1	40 D1
Kimberley Rd, Newcastle. ST5	39 F1
Kimberley St. ST3	48 D6
Kinder Pl. ST5	37 G3
King Charles Clo. ST3	56 B4
King George St. ST1	31 H4
King St, Chesterton. ST5	28 C1
King St, Cross Heath. ST5	29 E6
King St, Fenton. ST4	48 B1
King St, Newcastle. ST5	39 G3
King Edward St. ST3	49 E4
King William St. ST6	24 B2
Kingcross St. ST3	49 E4
Kingfisher Gro. ST6	25 G3
Kings Av. ST5	29 G4
Kings Croft. ST4	40 A3
Kings Pl. ST4	40 A2
Kings Rd. ST4	52 D1
Kings Ter. ST4	40 A2
Kingsbridge Av. ST5	45 G2
Kingsbury Gro. ST1	32 C2
Kingsclere Gro. ST1	32 A2
Kingsdale Clo. ST3	56 B3
Kingsdown Mews. ST5	45 G3
Kingsfield Oval. ST4	40 A2
Kingsfield Rd. ST4	40 A3
Kingsford Pl. ST3	56 C2
Kingside Gro. ST4	53 G6
Kingsland Av. ST4	46 C3
Kingsley St. ST3	56 C1
Kingsmead Rd. ST3	56 B4
Kingsnorth Pl. ST3	56 D4
Kingston Av. ST1	32 A2
Kingston Pl. ST6	26 B2
Kingsway. ST4	41 F5
Kingsway East. ST5	45 F1
Kingsway West. ST5	45 E1
Kingswell Rd. ST4	40 A3
Kingswinford Pl. ST6	31 H1
Kinsey St. ST5	37 G2
Kinver St. ST6	25 G4
Kipling Way. ST2	43 G2
Kirby St. ST6	31 E2
Kirk St. ST6	25 G4
Kirkbride Clo. ST3	49 G3
Kirkham St. ST4	41 E6
Kirkland La. ST4	40 D6
Kirkstall Pl. ST5	45 F3
Kirkup Walk. ST3	48 D4
Kirkwall Gro. ST2	27 E4
Kirsbrook Clo. ST4	53 G5
Kite Gro. ST3	56 C4
Knarsdale Clo. ST3	49 G2
Knight St. ST6	23 H1
Knights Croft. ST5	37 E5
Knowle St. ST4	41 E4
Knowle Wood Vw. ST3	48 B5
Knutton La. ST5	38 D2
Knutton Rd. ST5	29 H4
Knype Clo. ST5	29 E1
Knype Way. ST5	29 E1
Knypersley Rd. ST6	18 A5
Kyffin Rd. ST2	32 D2
Laburnum Clo. ST11	60 E3
Laburnum Gro. ST3	48 A4
Laburnum Pl, Crackley. ST5	22 B5
Laburnum Pl, Meir. ST3	56 A2
Lad La. ST5	39 G3
Ladybank Gro. ST3	54 A2
Ladysmith Rd. ST1	40 D1
Ladysmith St. ST3	48 D6
Ladywell Rd. ST6	24 A2
Lakewood Dri. ST12	59 G2
Lakewood Gro. ST1	30 D6
Lamb St. ST1	6 B3
Lambert St. ST6	24 B3
Lambourne Dri. ST2	27 F4
Lambourn Pl. ST5	54 A3
Lamerton Gro. ST3	50 A5
Lamotte Clo. ST4	49 E2
Lanark Walks. ST5	38 D5
Lancaster Av. ST5	39 H4
Lancaster Cres. ST4	40 A5
Lancaster Dri. ST6	26 B1
Lancaster Rd. ST5	39 H4
Lander Pl. ST6	17 F4
Landon St. ST3	49 F4
Landrake Gro. ST6	16 C3
Landseer Pl. ST5	28 C3
Lane Farm Gro. ST1	32 A1
Lanehead Rd. ST1	30 D6
Langdale Cres. ST1	31 H1
Langdale Rd. ST5	45 F2
Langford Rd. ST2	33 E6
Langford Rd. ST5	45 E4
Langham Rd. ST2	26 D4
Langland Dri. ST3	48 B6
Langley Clo. ST5	22 B4
Langley St. ST4	40 A2
Langton Ct. ST9	34 C4
Lansbury Gro. ST3	50 D5
Lansdell Av. ST5	29 F2
Lansdowne Cres. ST9	34 D4
Lansdowne Rd. ST4	40 B3
Lansdowne St. ST3	55 E1
Lapwing Clo. ST7	16 C1
Larch Gro. ST3	48 A5
Larch Pl. ST5	22 C5
Larchmount Clo. ST4	53 E4
Larkin Av. ST3	49 G3
Larksfield Rd. ST6	25 H5
Larkspur Gro. ST5	39 G1
Lascells St. ST6	24 A3
Laski Cres. ST3	50 D5
Latham Gro. ST	17 F3
Latimer Way. ST2	43 F2
Lauder Place Nth. ST2	43 H4
Lauder Place Sth. ST2	43 H5
Laurel Cres. ST9	34 C5
Laurel Gro. ST3	48 A5
Lauren Clo. ST4	42 B6
Lavender Av. ST11	60 D4
Lavender Clo. ST3	51 E2
Lawley St. ST3	49 G5
Lawn Farm Cres. ST2	43 G6
Lawrence St. ST1	41 F2
Lawson Ter. ST5	29 G3
Lawton St. ST6	25 E4
Laxey Rd. ST5	39 E1
Laxton Gro. ST4	58 D1
Lea Pl. ST3	50 D6
Leacroft Rd. ST3	56 B2
Leadbeater Av. ST4	46 D2
Leaford Walk. ST2	42 B2
Leaks Alley. ST3	49 E5
Leamington Gdns. ST5	30 B6
Leaside Rd. ST4	46 B2
Leason Rd. ST3	50 C5
Leason St. ST4	41 F5
Leaswood Clo. ST5	45 H5
Leaswood Pl. ST5	45 H6
Leawood Rd. ST4	46 B4
Ledbury Cres. ST1	32 B3
Ledstone Way. ST3	49 H4
Lee Gro. ST4	45 F4
Leech Av. ST5	29 E3
Leech St. ST5	39 H5
Leeds St. ST4	48 C2
Leek New Rd, Hanley. ST6	31 E2
Leek New Rd, Milton. ST1	26 C4
Leek Rd, Brown Edge. ST6	19 E3
Leek Rd, Cellarhead. ST9	35 G6
Leek Rd, Duke Bank. ST6	18 B6
Leek Rd, Endon. ST9	20 B3
Leek Rd, Milton. ST2	26 D6
Leek Rd, Northwood. ST1	32 B6
Leek Rd, Stockton Brook. ST9	19 G6
Leek Rd, Stoke. ST4	41 G4
Leek Rd, Weston Coyney. ST3	50 D1
Leese St. ST4	41 E5
Legge St. ST5	39 H5
Leicester Clo. ST5	45 H2
Leicester Pl. ST2	43 F1
Leigh La. ST6	23 G5
Leigh St. ST6	25 E4
Leighton Clo. ST9	27 F1
Lennox Rd. ST3	49 G6
Leonard Av, Baddeley Green. ST2	27 E2
Leonard Av, Hartshill. ST4	40 A4
Leonard Dri. ST6	19 E3
Leonard St. ST6	25 F4
Leonora St. ST6	30 D1
Leopold St. ST4	42 A6
Lessways Clo. ST5	23 F6
Lessways Walk. ST6	30 D1
Leveson Rd. ST4	52 C1
Leveson St. ST3	49 F6
Levita Rd. ST4	46 C3
Lewis St. ST4	41 E5
Lexham Pl. ST3	50 A5
Ley Gdns. ST3	48 D5
Leycett La. ST5	36 A3
Leyfield Rd. ST4	53 F5
Leyland Grn. ST6	17 E4
Leys Dri. ST5	44 D3
Leys La. ST2	27 F3
*Liberty La, Bradley Village. ST6	25 F2
Libra Pl. ST6	16 C4
Lichfield Clo. ST5	38 A2
Lichfield St. ST1	6 C4
Lidgate Gro. ST3	48 B5
Lidgate Walk. ST5	45 G6
Light Oaks Rd. ST2	27 G4
Lightwood Gro. ST2	26 C4
Lightwood Rd, Crackley. ST5	22 A5
Lightwood Rd, Florence. ST3	55 G1
Lightwood Rd, Longton. ST3	49 E5
Lilac Clo, Crackley. ST5	22 B5
Lilac Clo, Weston Coyney. ST3	51 E2
Lilac Gro. ST3	48 A4
Lilleshall Rd. ST5	45 H2
Lilleshall St. ST3	49 F6
Lillydale Rd. ST3	33 E6
Lily St. ST5	30 A3
Lime Clo. ST3	51 E2
Lime Gro. ST12	59 H1
Lime Heath Pl. ST6	16 B5
Limewood Clo. ST11	60 E3
Linacre Way. ST3	50 A2
Lincoln Av. ST5	45 H2
Lincoln Gro. ST5	45 G2
Lincoln Rd. ST6	30 D1
Lincoln St. ST1	31 H6
Linda Rd. ST6	16 B6
Lindale Gro. ST3	56 D4
Linden Clo. ST5	29 F6
Linden Gro. ST5	29 F6
Linden Pl. ST3	48 B6
Lindley Pl. ST3	55 G5
Lindley St. ST6	31 F1
Lindsay St. ST7	6 A6
Lindum Av. ST4	53 F4
Linfield Rd. ST1	31 H5
Lingard St. ST6	25 E6
Lingfield Av. ST6	18 D2
Linhope Gro. ST3	56 D4
Linkend Clo. ST1	32 C4
Links Av. ST5	29 F4
Linley Rd. ST4	40 B4
Linnburn Rd. ST3	49 G3
Linoop St. ST1	6 D3
Linwood Way. ST6	16 B6
Lion Gro. ST5	22 C6
Lion St. ST4	40 D6
Lionel Gro. ST4	40 B6
Lisbon Pl. ST5	38 D6
Liskeard Clo. ST2	42 C3
Little Chell La. ST6	16 C6
Little Cliffe Rd. ST3	48 B3
Little Eaves La. ST2	33 F2
Little Field. ST3	46 B3
Little La. ST3	55 E5
Little Row. ST4	42 B4
Liverpool Rd, Dimsdale. ST5	29 E4
Liverpool Rd, Newcastle. ST5	39 F3
Liverpool Rd, Red Street. ST5	22 B2
Liverpool Rd, Stoke. ST4	41 E5
Livingstone St. ST6	25 G4
Lloyd St. ST3	49 F6
Lockett St. ST1	31 H3
Locketts La. ST3	49 F6
Lockington Av. ST2	43 G2
Lockley St. ST1	32 A4
Lockwood St, Baddeley Green. ST5	27 G2
Lockwood St, Newcastle. ST2	40 A3
Lodge Gro. ST5	29 G3
Lodge Rd. ST4	40 B8
Loeley Pl. ST3	56 B3
Loftus St. ST1	6 A1
Loganbeck Gro. ST3	49 H2
Lomas St. ST4	41 E2
Lombardy Gro. ST3	50 B6
London Rd, Chesterton. ST5	28 C1
London Rd, Newcastle. ST5	39 G4
London Rd, Stoke. ST4	41 E6
London Rd, Trent Vale. ST4	46 C4

ong Mdw. ST5	45 G5	
ong Row. ST11	51 F4	
ongbridge Hayes Rd. ST6	23 H6	
ongbrook Av. ST3	48 C6	
ongclough Rd. ST5	22 B4	
ongdoles Av. ST3	50 A5	
ongfield Rd. ST4	40 B5	
ongford Walk. ST2	42 C2	
ongley Rd. ST3	49 E2	
ongnor Pl. ST2	42 D2	
ongport Rd. ST6	24 A6	
ongsdon Clo. ST5	22 A4	
ongsdon Gro. ST3	49 H3	
ongshaw Av. ST5	29 F2	
ongshaw St. ST6	24 A6	
ongton Hall Rd. ST3	48 B5	
ongton Rd, Barlaston. ST12	59 G5	
ongton Rd, Trentham. ST4	52 D5	
ongview Clo. ST3	49 G2	
onsdale St. ST4	41 F6	
oomer Rd. ST5	28 B4	
ord St. ST6	25 G4	
ordship La. ST4	41 G6	
ordship Pl. ST7	16 A1	
ordswood Rd. ST4	53 G4	
oring Rd. ST5	29 G3	
oring Ter Sth. ST5	29 G3	
orne St. ST6	25 E4	
orraine St. ST7	16 A1	
oughborough Wk. ST3	49 F3	
ouise Dri. ST3	48 B4	
ouise St. ST6	25 E4	
ouvain Av. ST1	31 H1	
ovage Gro. ST2	32 D6	
ovatt Av. ST5	29 E5	
ovatt St. ST4	41 E5	
oveston Gro. ST3	49 G3	
owe St. ST4	41 F6	
owell Dri. ST3	50 A3	
ower Bedford St. ST4	41 E2	
ower Bethesda St. ST1	6 C6	
ower Bryan St. ST1	6 B1	
ower Cres. ST4	40 B4	
ower Foundry St. ST1	6 B3	
ower Hadderidge. ST6	30 C1	
ower Mayer St. ST1	31 H4	
ower Milehouse La. ST5	28 D6	
ower Oxford Rd. ST5	40 B1	
ower Spring Rd. ST3	49 G6	
ower St, Burslem. ST6	30 D1	
ower St, Newcastle. ST5	39 F3	
owfield Dri. ST5	30 B3	
owhurst St. ST6	16 D3	
owlands Rd. ST7	23 F1	
owndes Clo. ST4	46 C1	
owther St. ST1	31 E4	
owthorne Way. ST2	43 H3	
ucas St. ST6	24 B6	
ucerne Pl. ST5	38 C6	
udbrook Rd. ST4	49 E2	
udford Clo. ST5	22 B4	
udlow St. ST1	31 H6	
udwall Rd. ST3	55 H1	
ugano Clo. ST5	38 D6	
uke St. ST6	30 C2	
ukes Land Av. ST4	40 B6	
ulworth Gro. ST6	16 C4	
undy Rd. ST3	48 C4	
unford Pl. ST3	50 A5	
undia Dri. ST1	32 B2	
unham St. ST4	41 E5	
une Dri. ST5	46 A2	
une Gro. ST6	29 G6	
une Rd. ST3	56 D1	
une Valley Rd. ST5	39 G5	
une Wood Gro. ST5	39 F5	
unebrook Cres. ST4	46 B5	
unes Rd, Keele. ST5	37 E6	
unes Rd, Seabridge. ST5	44 A4	
unemewood Clo. ST5	39 F5	
unminster Gro. ST2	27 E4	
unvale Rd. ST4	46 B3	
undhurst St. ST6	24 C6	
unmouth Gro. ST6	16 C3	
unn St. ST3	50 D1	

Lynton Gro. ST3	56 A3	
Lynton Rd. ST5	45 E2	
Lysander Rd. ST3	56 C4	
Lytton St. ST4	41 F5	
Macclesfield St. ST6	24 E5	
Macdonald Cres. ST3	50 C5	
Mace St. ST4	46 C4	
Machin Cres. ST5	29 F1	
Machin St. ST6	24 B1	
Macintyre St. ST6	30 D1	
Maclagan St. ST4	41 F6	
Maddock St. ST6	24 B6	
Madeley St, Silverdale. ST5	37 H2	
Madeley St, Tunstall. ST6	24 A1	
Madison St. ST6	24 A1	
Mafeking St. ST3	48 D6	
Magdalen Rd. ST3	54 A2	
Magdalen Walk. ST3	54 A3	
Magenta Dri. ST6	38 C1	
Magnolia Dri. ST6	26 B3	
Magnus St. ST6	30 C1	
Maidstone Gro. ST2	43 F1	
Main St. ST3	50 D2	
Maitland Gro. ST4	53 F5	
Malam St. ST1	6 A1	
Malcolm Clo. ST2	26 D3	
Malcolm Dri. ST2	33 F4	
Malham Rd. ST5	38 C1	
Malkin Way. ST6	30 C2	
Mallard Way. ST6	25 G3	
Mallorie Rd. ST6	17 H6	
Mallowdale Clo. ST4	53 G4	
Malstone Av. ST2	27 E3	
Malt La. ST3	49 G5	
Malthouse La. ST12	59 G4	
Malthouse Rd. ST2	42 D1	
Malton Gro. ST6	16 A6	
Malvern Av. ST5	37 E2	
Malvern Clo. ST4	52 D3	
Mandella Way. ST3	49 F6	
Mandeville Clo. ST6	25 F3	
Manifold Clo. ST5	37 G3	
Manifold Rd. ST11	60 D2	
Manifold Walk. ST2	43 F3	
Mann St. ST3	51 E5	
Mannim Clo. ST3	50 B3	
Manor Court St. ST4	40 D6	
Manor St. ST4	42 A6	
Manse Clo. ST3	49 F3	
Mansfield Clo. ST5	45 H6	
Maple Av. ST5	22 B5	
Maple Clo. ST6	18 C5	
Maple Cres. ST11	60 E3	
Maple Pl. ST3	50 D6	
Maplehurst St. ST6	25 F6	
Marcel Clo. ST4	47 E6	
March Rd. ST3	49 E3	
Marchwood Ct. ST4	46 B1	
Margaret Av. ST4	52 C2	
Margaret St. ST1	3 A5	
Margill Clo. ST1	41 F1	
Maries Way. ST6	38 B3	
Marina Dri. ST5	29 H5	
Marina Way. ST1	30 D6	
Marina Rd. ST4	46 C4	
Marino Clo. ST3	55 F2	
Market La, Hanley. ST1	6 C3	
Market La, Newcastle. ST5	39 G3	
Market Pass. ST6	24 C6	
Market Pl. ST6	24 C6	
Market Sq. ST1	31 G5	
Market Sq Av. ST1	6 C3	
Market St. ST3	49 E4	
Marlborough Gro. ST9	20 B1	
Marlborough Rd. ST3	49 E3	
Marlborough St. ST4	47 H2	
Marlow Clo. ST3	49 G2	
Marlow Rd. ST3	49 G2	
Marney Walk. ST6	25 F4	
Marriott St. ST4	48 D2	
Mars St. ST6	25 G5	
Marsden St. ST1	31 H5	
Marsh Av, Dimsdale. ST5	29 H3	
Marsh Av, Smallthorne. ST6	25 F4	
Marsh Gro. ST9	34 C4	
Marsh Par. ST5	39 H4	

Marsh St Nth. ST1	6 A2	
Marsh St Sth. ST1	6 B3	
Marsh View. ST3	55 G5	
Marsh Way. ST5	29 G4	
Marshall Av. ST6	19 E3	
Marshall St. ST6	24 C4	
Marshland Gro. ST6	17 E2	
Marston Gro. ST1	25 H6	
Martin St. ST6	31 F1	
Martindale Clo. ST3	56 B2	
Marychurch Rd. ST2	32 D6	
Maryrose Clo. ST2	33 E6	
Masefield Rd. ST3	48 C6	
Mason St. ST4	48 B2	
Masterson St. ST4	47 H1	
Mathews Walk. ST1	6 D3	
Matlock Pl. ST5	37 F2	
Matlock St. ST1	41 G2	
Maud St. ST4	42 A6	
Maunders Rd. ST2	26 C4	
Maureen Gro. ST5	29 H5	
Mawdesley St. ST6	31 E2	
Mawson Gro. ST1	41 G3	
Maxton Way. ST3	50 D5	
Maxwell Pl. ST4	40 B5	
May Av, Basford. ST6	40 A1	
May Av, Tunstall. ST6	24 C2	
May Pl, Basford. ST5	39 H1	
May Pl, Longton. ST4	49 E3	
May St, Silverdale. ST5	37 H2	
May St, Stanfield. ST6	25 E4	
Maybury Way. ST2	26 D4	
Mayer Av. ST5	39 F1	
Mayer St. ST1	6 C1	
Mayfair Gro. ST9	20 B1	
Mayfield Av, Newcastle. ST5	39 E4	
Mayfield Av, Northwood. ST1	32 B4	
Mayfield Cres. ST1	32 B4	
Mayfield Dri. ST11	57 F3	
Mayfield Pl. ST5	29 H6	
Mayfield Pl East. ST4	46 B3	
Mayfield Pl West. ST4	46 B2	
Maylea Cres. ST6	31 G1	
Mayne St. ST4	46 C6	
Mayneford Pl. ST4	52 C1	
Maythorne Rd. ST3	54 C1	
McGough St. ST6	24 A2	
Meadow Av, Dimsdale. ST5	29 E5	
Meadow Av, Florence. ST3	55 F2	
Meadow Clo, Blythe Brook. ST11	57 G4	
Meadow Clo, Forsbrook. ST11	60 F1	
Meadow Dri. ST3	54 C3	
Meadow La, Dimsdale. ST5	29 E6	
Meadow La, Trentham. ST4	53 F3	
Meadow Pl. ST3	50 D6	
Meadow Rd, Barlaston. ST12	59 E5	
Meadow Rd, Brown Edge. ST6	19 E4	
Meadow Rd, Gt Chell. ST6	17 F5	
Meadow Side. ST4	53 F4	
Meadow St, Broad Meadow. ST3	28 D3	
Meadow St, Milton. ST2	26 D4	
Meadowcroft Grn. ST11	57 E2	
Meadowview. ST2	26 A2	
Meaford Dri. ST3	48 A5	
Meaford Rd. ST12	59 E6	
Meakin Av. ST3	45 F4	
Meakins Row. ST4	48 C2	
Medway Pl. ST5	45 F3	
Medway Walk. ST6	24 D1	
Meerbrook Clo. ST4	53 F6	
Meere Clo. ST6	26 B2	
Meigh Rd. ST9	34 B5	
Meigh St. ST1	6 C3	
Meiklejohn Pl. ST6	17 E4	
Meir Rd. ST3	49 H6	
Meir View. ST3	50 C6	
Meirhay Rd. ST3	49 G5	
Melbourne St. ST3	49 G2	

Melchester Gro. ST3	56 A1	
Melfont St. ST6	24 C3	
Meliden Way. ST4	40 C6	
Mellard St. ST5	39 F2	
Mellor St. ST7	16 A1	
Melrose Av, Meir Heath. ST3	55 G5	
Melrose Av, Sneyd Green. ST1	31 H1	
Melrose Av, Westlands. ST5	45 F2	
Melstone Av. ST6	24 C2	
Melville Ct. ST5	44 B5	
Melville Rd. ST3	49 H6	
Melville St. ST1	42 A1	
Melvyn Cres. ST5	29 H1	
Menai Gro. ST3	49 F2	
Mendip Pl. ST5	28 C6	
Mendip Grn. ST2	26 C5	
Mercer St. ST3	55 E1	
Mercia Cres. ST6	30 D2	
Mercury Pl. ST6	25 G5	
Meremore Dri. ST5	22 B4	
Merevale Av. ST2	42 D2	
Meriden Rd. ST5	45 H6	
Merlin Clo. ST6	16 D2	
Merrial St. ST5	39 G3	
Merrick St. ST1	31 H3	
Merrion Dri. ST6	25 F3	
Mersey Rd. ST5	45 F4	
Mersey St. ST1	6 A4	
Merton St. ST3	49 F3	
Metcalfe Rd. ST6	24 D2	
Mews Clo. ST2	42 D2	
Michael Clo. ST5	50 D4	
Michaels Clo. ST5	29 H2	
Michigan Gro. ST4	53 F2	
Mickleby Way. ST3	57 E4	
Middle Cross St. ST3	49 F3	
Middlefield Rd. ST2	43 G4	
Middleton Clo. ST6	26 B2	
Midhurst Clo. ST7	16 C2	
Midway Dri. ST11	57 H4	
Mier St. ST6	24 B1	
Milan Dri. ST5	38 C6	
Milborne Dri. ST5	45 G1	
Milburn Rd. ST6	31 F2	
Mile Ct. ST5	38 D1	
Miles Bank. ST1	6 B3	
Milford Av. ST9	34 D4	
Milford Rd. ST6	39 E5	
Milford St. ST4	48 C2	
Milgreen Av. ST1	31 H1	
Mill Clo. ST11	51 F4	
Mill Hayes Rd. ST6	24 B4	
Mill Hill Cres. ST6	24 D1	
Mill La. ST9	35 G1	
Mill St. ST5	38 A2	
Mill View. ST6	17 H5	
Millbank Pl. ST5	38 D3	
Millbank St. ST3	49 F4	
Millbridge Clo. ST3	56 C5	
Millbrook Gro. ST2	26 C4	
Millennium Way. ST5	22 B3	
Miller St. ST5	39 H3	
Millers La. ST2	26 C4	
Millet Rd. ST2	32 C6	
Millfield Cres. ST2	26 D4	
Millicent St. ST4	42 A6	
Millrise Rd. ST2	26 D5	
Millward Gro. ST3	56 B5	
Millward Rd. ST2	33 F6	
Milnes Clo. ST3	48 C5	
Milton Rd. ST1	26 A6	
Milton St. ST1	41 E1	
Milvale St. ST6	30 B1	
Milverton Pl. ST3	48 C5	
Minard Gro. ST3	50 B3	
Minden Gro. ST6	25 H6	
Mineral Rd. ST2	43 F5	
Minerva Rd. ST4	48 B1	
Minshall St. ST4	47 G2	
Minster St. ST6	25 E4	
Minton Pl. ST5	30 A3	
Minton St, Hartshill. ST4	40 C4	
Minton St, Wolstanton. ST5	30 A4	
Miranda Gro. ST6	25 H5	
Mitchell St. ST6	24 C4	
Moffat Gro. ST2	43 H5	

74

ark Rd,
Silverdale. ST5 — 37 H3
ark Rd,
Stanfield. ST6 — 25 E4
ark Rd,
Werrington. ST9 — 35 E4
ark St. ST4 — 48 B1
ark Ter. ST6 — 24 B2
ark Vw. ST11 — 57 G5
ark Way. ST11 — 60 E2
arker Jervis Rd. ST3 — 50 B3
arker St. ST1 — 6 A4
arkfield Rd. ST3 — 55 F2
arkfields. ST9 — 20 C2
arkfields Clo,
Barlaston. ST12 — 59 E6
arkfields Clo, Keele. ST5 — 37 F2
arkhead Dri. ST3 — 50 C4
arkhead Gro. ST3 — 50 C4
arkhouse Rd East. ST5 — 22 D5
arkhouse Rd West. ST5 — 22 C5
arkside. ST4 — 53 E3
arkside Cres. ST9 — 20 C1
arkside Dri. ST5 — 40 A1
arkside Gro. ST5 — 40 A1
arkstone Av. ST5 — 39 H5
arkwood Av. ST4 — 52 C3
arliament Row. ST1 — 6 C3
arliament Sq. ST1 — 6 C3
arsonage St. ST6 — 24 A1
arton Gro ST3 — 50 C4
artridge Clo. ST3 — 56 C4
atterdale St. ST6 — 25 E2
avillion Dri. ST1 — 31 E4
axton St. ST1 — 41 H1
aynter St. ST4 — 48 C1
eacehaven Gro. ST4 — 53 F6
eacock Hay Rd. ST7 — 22 C1
eacock Rd. ST5 — 29 E4
eacock View. ST4 — 42 B3
eake St. ST5 — 38 C1
ear Pl. ST2 — 43 G5
ear Tree Clo. ST12 — 59 E5
ear Tree La. ST5 — 22 B5
earl Gro. ST3 — 56 B3
eascroft Rd. ST6 — 17 H6
ebble Mill St. ST1 — 30 D6
eck Mill La. ST8 — 17 F1
edley St. ST3 — 54 B3
edley Gro. ST6 — 25 H5
eebles Grn. ST2 — 43 F2
eebles Rd. ST5 — 37 E1
eel St, Dresden. ST3 — 55 E1
eel St,
Longbridge Hayes. ST6 — 23 H6
eels St. ST5 — 29 H4
egasus Gro. ST6 — 25 H4
egroy Gro. ST6 — 25 H4
elham St. ST1 — 6 D6
emberton Dri. ST3 — 55 F4
embridge Rd. ST3 — 54 A3
embroke Dri. ST5 — 39 E5
embroke Rd. ST2 — 26 D4
enarth Gro. ST1 — 31 F4
enarth Pl. ST5 — 39 E5
endine Gro. ST4 — 49 E1
enfleet Av. ST3 — 56 C1
engrove Clo. ST6 — 16 B2
enk Rd. ST11 — 60 E2
enkhull Ct. ST4 — 41 E5
enkhull New Rd. ST4 — 40 D6
enkhull Ter. ST4 — 40 D6
enkville St. ST4 — 46 D2
enmark Gro. ST3 — 56 A2
enmere Dri,
Werrington. ST9 — 34 C5
enmere Dri,
Westbury Park. ST5 — 44 B5
ennell St. ST2 — 33 E6
ennine Way. ST5 — 28 C6
ennington Clo. ST3 — 51 E6
ennyfields Av. ST6 — 24 A4
ennymore Clo. ST4 — 53 E3
enport Gro. ST3 — 48 D6
enrhyn Av. ST6 — 25 F4
enrith Clo. ST4 — 53 G5
enrith Ct. ST5 — 45 G1
ensford Gro. ST1 — 32 B4
entland Gro. ST5 — 28 C6
enton Pl. ST3 — 54 A3
enton Walk. ST3 — 54 A3

Pepper St,
Keele. ST5 — 36 D4
Pepper St,
Newcastle. ST5 — 39 G4
Pepper St,
Silverdale. ST5 — 37 E3
Perceval St. ST1 — 32 A4
Percival Dri. ST9 — 27 F2
Percy St. ST1 — 6 C3
Peregrine Gro. ST3 — 56 C4
Perivale Clo. ST1 — 32 C3
Perry Clo. ST1 — 6 D4
Perrymount Ct. ST4 — 46 C1
Persia Walk. ST6 — 24 A2
Perth St. ST4 — 48 D2
Perthy Gro. ST4 — 52 D3
Perton Wood View. ST3 — 48 B5
Petersfield Rd. ST6 — 16 D3
Petrel Gro. ST3 — 56 D4
Pevensey Gro. ST3 — 49 F1
Philip La. ST9 — 34 D4
Philip St. ST4 — 48 B1
Phillipson Way. ST6 — 25 H5
Phoenix St. ST6 — 24 A2
Picasso Rise. ST3 — 56 D4
Piccadilly. ST1 — 6 B4
Piccadilly Arc. ST1 — 6 B3
Piccadilly Sq. ST1 — 6 C3
Piccadilly St. ST6 — 24 A2
Pickering Clo. ST3 — 54 D1
Pickford Pl. ST3 — 56 B1
Pickmere Clo. ST2 — 27 E2
Picton St. ST1 — 31 H6
Pidduck St. ST6 — 30 B1
Pierce St. ST6 — 24 A2
Piggott Gro. ST2 — 32 D6
Pilkington Av. ST5 — 45 F1
Pillar Clo. ST2 — 43 G5
Pilsbury St. ST5 — 30 A3
Pilsden Pl. ST3 — 57 E4
Pine Ct. ST11 — 57 F3
Pine Rd. ST4 — 47 G3
Pinehurst Clo. ST5 — 45 F5
Pinetree Dri. ST11 — 57 F3
Pinewood Cres. ST3 — 50 D6
Pinewood Gro,
Blythe Bridge. ST11 — 60 E3
Pinewood Gro,
Crackley. ST5 — 22 C5
Pinfold Av. ST6 — 26 A1
Pinhoe Pl. ST3 — 49 H4
Pinnox St. ST6 — 24 B3
Pireford Pl. ST5 — 23 F4
Pirehill Rd. ST5 — 23 F5
Pitcairn St. ST6 — 24 B2
Pitfield Av. ST5 — 30 A6
Pitgreen La. ST5 — 30 A3
Pitlea Pl. ST3 — 49 F1
Pitsford St. ST3 — 49 H5
Pitt St East. ST6 — 24 D6
Pitts Hill Bank. ST6 — 16 C6
Plainfield Gro. ST3 — 43 G4
Plane Gro. ST5 — 22 C5
Plant St. ST3 — 49 F3
Plantation Rd. ST4 — 53 H4
Platts Av. ST9 — 20 B3
Pleasant St. ST6 — 30 C1
Plex St. ST6 — 24 A2
Pleydell St. ST1 — 26 B6
Plough St. ST1 — 31 H4
Plumtree Gro. ST1 — 32 C2
Plymouth Gro. ST5 — 28 D1
Pochard Clo. ST6 — 25 G3
Podmore St. ST6 — 31 E1
Pointon Gro. ST6 — 18 C5
Polperro Way. ST3 — 56 C4
Pomona Rise. ST1 — 25 H6
Pool Dam. ST5 — 39 F4
Pool St, Newcastle. ST5 — 39 F4
Pool St,
Sandford Hill. ST4 — 48 D1
Poole Av. ST3 — 27 E3
Poolfield Av. ST5 — 39 E4
Poolfields Clo. ST5 — 38 D4
Poolfields Ct,
Brown Edge. ST6 — 19 E3
Poolfields Ct,
Longton. ST3 — 49 E4
Poolhill Clo. ST3 — 48 D6
Poolside, Blurton. ST3 — 54 B2
Poolside,
Newcastle. ST5 — 39 F3

Poplar Av. ST5 — 29 E6
Poplar Clo,
Blythe Bridge. ST11 — 60 D3
Poplar Clo,
Cross Heath. ST5 — 29 E6
Poplar Ct. ST5 — 29 F6
Poplar Dri. ST3 — 48 B6
Poplar Gro, Blurton. ST3 — 54 C1
Poplar Gro,
Newcastle. ST5 — 39 H3
Porlock Gro. ST4 — 53 F5
Port St. ST6 — 30 B1
Port Vale St. ST6 — 24 B6
Porthill Bank. ST5 — 29 H2
Porthill Grange. ST5 — 29 H2
Porthill Grn. ST5 — 29 H2
Porthill Rd. ST6 — 30 A1
Portland Clo. ST11 — 57 F4
Portland Cres. ST11 — 60 F1
Portland Gro. ST5 — 45 G4
Portland Mews. ST5 — 29 G3
Portland Pl. ST12 — 59 H1
Portland Rd. ST3 — 49 E3
Portland St. ST1 — 31 F4
Post La. ST9 — 20 C3
Potteries Way. ST1 — 6 A1
Poulson St. ST4 — 41 E6
Pound Gdns. ST6 — 25 H1
Poundsgate Gro ST4 — 53 E3
Povey Pl. ST5 — 23 F5
Povey St. ST6 — 24 C6
Powderham Clo. ST6 — 16 B2
Powell St. ST1 — 31 E4
Power Gro. ST3 — 48 D4
Prestbury Av. ST5 — 45 G6
Preston St. ST6 — 25 G5
Pretoria Rd. ST1 — 40 D1
Priam Clo. ST1 — 23 F5
Price St. ST6 — 24 D5
Priestley Dri. ST3 — 49 G3
Prime St. ST1 — 32 A4
Primitive St. ST4 — 25 H4
Primrose Gro. ST5 — 39 G1
Primrose Hill. ST4 — 47 E6
Princes Rd. ST4 — 40 C4
Princess Dri. ST3 — 50 C4
Princess Sq. ST6 — 24 A6
Princess St,
Newcastle. ST5 — 39 H3
Princess St,
Tunstall. ST6 — 24 A3
Princetown Clo. ST3 — 56 C4
Priorfield Clo. ST3 — 49 E3
Priory Rd,
Abbey Hulton. ST2 — 33 E2
Priory Rd,
Newcastle. ST5 — 39 F6
Probyn St. ST3 — 49 E6
Prospect Pl. ST4 — 46 C4
Prospect St. ST6 — 30 B2
Prospect Ter. ST5 — 39 F3
Providence St. ST1 — 31 H3
Pump Bank. ST5 — 37 E5
Pump St, Newcastle. ST5 — 39 F4
Pump St, Stoke. ST4 — 41 E5
Purbeck St. ST6 — 31 F2
Purser Cres. ST5 — 29 G4
Pyenest St. ST1 — 41 E2

Quadrant Rd. ST1 — 6 B2
Quail Gro. ST3 — 56 C4
Quarry Av. ST4 — 40 D4
Quarry Bank Rd. ST5 — 37 E4
Quarry Clo,
Stockton Brook. ST9 — 27 F2
Quarry Clo,
Werrington. ST9 — 34 C4
Quarry Rd. ST4 — 40 D5
Queen Anne St. ST4 — 41 F4
Queen St. ST5 — 39 G3
*Queen Elizabeth II Ct,
Temple St. ST4 — 47 H1
Queen Mary Rd. ST4 — 46 D6
Queen Marys Dri. ST12 — 59 G2
Queen St, Burslem. ST6 — 24 C6
Queen St,
Chesterton. ST5 — 28 C1
Queen St,
Newcastle. ST5 — 39 G3
Queen St, Porthill. ST5 — 29 G2
Queens Av. ST6 — 24 C2

Queens Ct. ST1 — 32 A5
Queens Park Av. ST3 — 54 D1
Queens Rd. ST4 — 40 C5
Queens Row. ST12 — 59 H4
Queens Walk. ST3 — 50 C4
Queens Way. ST5 — 45 F1
Queensberry Rd. ST3 — 49 G6
Queensmead Rd. ST3 — 56 A3
Queensway,
Boothen. ST4 — 47 F3
Queensway,
Etruria. ST5 — 40 B1
Quinton Gro. ST5 — 29 G5
Quinton Walk. ST6 — 25 G3

Race Course. ST5 — 38 A3
Racecourse Rd. ST4 — 46 D3
Rachel Gro. ST4 — 49 E1
Radford Rd. ST4 — 40 C3
Radley Way. ST9 — 34 D4
Radstone Rise. ST5 — 45 F5
Raglan St. ST4 — 47 H1
Railton Av. ST3 — 54 C1
Railway Ct. ST9 — 20 C2
Railway Pass. ST3 — 49 F4
Railway St. ST6 — 24 B3
Railway Ter. ST5 — 49 G4
Rainford Clo. ST7 — 16 A1
Rainham Gro. ST6 — 17 E1
Ralph Dri. ST1 — 26 B6
Ramage Gro. ST3 — 55 G1
Ramsey Clo. ST12 — 59 G1
Ramsey Rd. ST5 — 39 E1
Ramsey St. ST4 — 47 G2
Ramshaw Gro. ST3 — 49 G1
Ranelagh St. ST1 — 6 B6
Rangemore Ter. ST5 — 30 A6
Ransome Pl. ST3 — 50 A3
Ranworth Clo. ST5 — 45 F6
Rathbone Av. ST5 — 30 A6
Rathbone St. ST6 — 24 B2
Rattigan Dri. ST3 — 50 B3
Ratton St. ST1 — 6 D2
Ravenna Way. ST — 49 H3
Ravenswood Clo. ST5 — 45 F4
Rawlins St. ST1 — 32 A4
Rayleigh Way. ST2 — 43 G3
Raymond Av. ST1 — 31 H1
Raymond St. ST1 — 41 F1
Reading Way. ST2 — 43 G1
Reads Row. ST4 — 42 B4
Rebecca St. ST4 — 41 E5
Recorder Gro. ST3 — 17 F4
Recreation Rd. ST1 — 49 H6
Rectory Pass. ST1 — 41 F1
Rectory Rd. ST1 — 41 E2
Rectory St. ST1 — 41 E1
Red House Cres. ST3 — 48 D4
Red La. ST2 — 27 F4
Red Lion Pass. ST1 — 6 A6
Redbridge Clo. ST4 — 52 C1
Redcar Rd. ST4 — 53 E3
Redheath Clo. ST5 — 37 E2
Redhills Rd. ST2 — 26 C6
Redlands Dri. ST2 — 33 G6
Redman Gro. ST6 — 31 G1
Redmine Clo. ST5 — 29 E4
Redwood Pl. ST3 — 56 B1
Reedbed Gro. ST6 — 25 G2
Reedham Way. ST2 — 43 G2
Reeves Av, Bank Top. ST6 — 25 E2
Reeves Av, May Bank. ST5 — 29 F6
*Refinery St,
Stubbs Bank. ST5 — 39 G4
Regency Dri. ST2 — 27 E4
Regent Av. ST6 — 24 C2
Regent Ct. ST5 — 29 G2
Regent Rd. ST1 — 6 C6
Regent St. ST4 — 46 D2
Regina St. ST6 — 25 H3
Reginald Mitchell Way.
ST1 — 23 G1
Reginald St. ST6 — 24 D5
Registry St. ST4 — 41 F5
Reid St. ST6 — 24 B6
Rembrandt Way. ST3 — 56 D4
Remer St. ST6 — 31 E3
Renfrew Clo. ST5 — 38 D5
Renfrew Pl. ST4 — 52 D1
Renown Clo. ST2 — 42 C3
Repington Rd. ST1 — 26 B6

Name	Ref		Name	Ref		Name	Ref		Name	Ref
Repton Dri. ST5	44 D2		Rosevean Clo. ST1	6 A1		St Bernard Pl. ST2	32 D4		Sandy Hill. ST9	35 E
Reservoir Rd. ST3	49 H6		Rosewood Av. ST9	27 F1		St Bernards Rd. ST5	38 D1		Sandy La,	
Reynard Walk. ST3	56 D4		Ross Clo. ST3	50 B3		St Chads Rd. ST6	24 C2		Baddeley Edge. ST2	27 F
Reynolds Av. ST5	28 C2		Ross Clo. ST3	44 D3		St Christopher Av. ST4	40 B6		Sandy La, Basford. ST5	39 H
Reynolds Rd. ST6	24 D2		Rossett Gro. ST6	16 C2		St Clair St. ST3	49 F6		Sandy La,	
Rhodes Ct. ST5	29 H2		Rosslyn Rd. ST3	49 F5		St Edmunds Av. ST5	30 A2		Brown Edge. ST6	19 E
Rhodes St. ST1	31 H3		Rosy Bank. ST9	27 F2		St Georges Av Nth.			Sandyfield Rd. ST1	32 A
Rhondda Av. ST6	31 G1		Rother Walk. ST6	25 E1		ST5	29 G4		Sangster La. ST6	25 H
Ribble Clo. ST5	45 F4		Rothesay Av. ST5	38 D5		St Georges Av West.			Sant St. ST6	24 B
Ricardo St. ST3	55 E1		Rothesay Ct. ST5	38 D5		ST5	29 G4		Saracen Way. ST3	56 C
Riceyman Rd. ST5	23 F5		Rothesay Rd. ST3	49 G6		St Georges Av,			Sargeant Av. ST6	16 D
Richards Av. ST6	24 C2		Rothley Grn. ST3	54 B3		Bank Top. ST6	25 E1		Sark Clo. ST5	44 C
Richardson Pl. ST6	17 F4		Rothsay Av. ST1	26 A6		St Georges Av,			Sark Pl. ST3	49 G
Richmond Av. ST1	25 H6		Rothwell St. ST4	46 D1		Dimsdale. ST5	29 G4		Saturn Rd. ST6	25 G
Richmond Gro. ST5	40 B1		Rotterdam. ST5	39 E3		St Georges Av,			Saunders Rd. ST5	29 F
Richmond Rd. ST1	52 D1		Rotterdam Rd. ST5	38 D3		Endon. ST9	20 B3		*Scarlett St,	
Richmond Rd. ST4	40 D4		Roughcote La. ST11	51 E1		St Georges Cres. ST4	52 D1		Market La. ST5	39 G
Richmond Ter. ST1	41 F2		Roundfields. ST9	27 F2		St Georges Rd. ST5	39 E4		Scarratt Clo. ST11	60 F
Ridge Clo. ST12	59 E6		Roundway. ST3	48 A5		St Giles Rd. ST5	38 D2		Scarratt Dri. ST11	60 F
Ridge Cres. ST3	56 B5		Rowan Gro. ST3	48 A5		St Gregorys Rd. ST3	48 D5		Sceptre St. ST1	6 A
Ridge Walk. ST3	56 A3		Rowan Pl. ST5	22 C5		St Helier Clo. ST5	44 D4		School La,	
Ridgehouse Dri. ST1	30 D4		Rowandale. ST3	49 G2		St James Pl. ST4	52 D1		Blurton. ST3	54 C
Ridgmont Rd. ST4	44 D4		Rowhurst Clo. ST5	28 B2		St James St. ST1	6 A5		School La,	
Ridgway Dri. ST11	57 F4		Rowhurst Pl. ST6	17 F6		St John St. ST1	6 D1		Cookshill. ST11	51 F
Ridgway Pl. ST5	30 A3		Rowland St. ST3	55 E1		St Johns Av,			School Rd. ST2	32 D
Ridgway Rd. ST4	41 G3		Rowley Av. ST5	28 D1		May Bank. ST5	29 H5		School St,	
Ridley St. ST4	47 G2		Rownall Pl. ST3	50 C6		St Johns Av,			Chesterton. ST5	28 D
Riley Av. ST6	25 F3		Rownall Rd, Meir. ST3	50 C6		Trent Vale. ST4	46 B4		School St,	
Riley St Nth. ST6	24 C6		Rownall Rd,			St Johns Pl. ST5	38 D1		Newcastle. ST5	39 G
Riley St Sth. ST6	24 C6		Werrington. ST9	35 F4		St Johns Sq. ST6	24 C6		School St,	
Rill St. ST4	49 E3		Roxburghe Av. ST3	49 F6		St Lucys Dri. ST5	29 G2		Trent Vale. ST4	46 C
Rimini Clo. ST3	49 H2		Royal St. ST4	48 D2		St Luke St. ST1	31 H6		Scot Hay Rd. ST5	36 D
Ringland Clo. ST1	31 H5		Roycroft Clo. ST5	23 G6		St Lukes Clo. ST5	37 G2		Scotia Rd. ST6	24 B
Ripon Av. ST5	28 C1		Royden Av. ST1	32 B5		St Margarets Ct. ST5	30 A4		Scott Lidgett Rd. ST6	24 A
Ripon Rd. ST3	54 B3		Roylance St. ST6	24 A2		St Margarets Dri. ST1	26 A6		Scott Rd. ST6	16 D
Riseley Rd. ST4	40 B4		Royston Walk. ST3	49 F4		St Margarets Gro. ST3	48 B5		Scragg St. ST7	16 C
Rists Rd. ST5	29 E5		Royville Pl. ST6	25 H5		St Marks Clo. ST1	41 F1		Scrimshaw Dri. ST6	25 F
Riverdale Dri. ST6	16 B2		Rubens Way. ST3	56 D4		St Marks St. ST1	41 F1		Scrivener Rd. ST4	40 C
Riverhead Clo. ST6	18 C6		Rubian St. ST4	48 B1		St Martins Rd. ST5	39 E4		Seabridge La. ST5	44 C
Riverside Rd. ST4	46 B5		Rudyard Gro. ST5	29 H5		St Marys Dri. ST5	39 E4		Seabridge Rd. ST5	39 F
Riversmead. ST5	45 G4		Rugby Clo. ST5	44 D3		St Marys Rd,			Seaford St. ST4	41 F
Rivington Cres. ST6	17 E4		Rugby Dri. ST3	55 E2		Sandford. ST3	49 G2		Seagrave Pl. ST5	45 E
Rixdale Clo. ST1	31 G4		Runnymede Clo. ST2	32 D6		St Marys Rd,			Seagrave St. ST5	39 H
Robert Heath St. ST6	25 G4		Rushcliffe Dri. ST3	56 C4		Wolstanton. ST5	30 A3		Seaton Clo. ST3	56 A
Robert St. ST6	24 A1		Rushmoor Gro. ST3	56 D4		St Mathews Ct. ST4	48 C1		Sebring Av. ST3	55 H
Roberts Av. ST5	39 F1		Rushton Clo. ST6	19 E3		St Matthew St. ST4	48 C1		Second Av,	
Robertson Dri. ST5	28 D6		Rushton Gro. ST6	31 E2		St Michaels Rd,			Brookhouse Lane. ST2	33 H
Robertson Sq. ST4	46 C3		Rushton Rd. ST6	31 E2		Great Chell. ST6	16 C5		Second Av,	
Robin Croft. ST6	24 D6		Rushton Way. ST11	60 E2		St Michaels Rd,			Porthill. ST5	29 G
Robin Hill Gro. ST4	49 E2		Ruskin Clo. ST3	49 G3		Newcastle. ST5	39 F1		Sedbergh Clo. ST3	44 D
Robinson Av. ST6	25 H6		Russell Gro. ST9	32 C2		St Nicholas Av. ST6	18 A6		Seddon Rd. ST3	56 A
Robinson Ct. ST3	54 B2		Russett Clo. ST9	34 D4		St Patricks Dri. ST5	38 D4		Sedgley Walk. ST3	49 F
Robinson Rd. ST4	52 C3		Russell St,			St Pauls Ct. ST3	48 C5		Seedfields Rd. ST3	48 A
Robson St. ST1	6 A5		Dimsdale. ST5	29 H4		St Pauls Rd. ST5	39 E3		Sefton Av. ST1	32 A
Rochester Rd. ST3	49 E2		Russell St, Dresden. ST3	55 E1		St Pauls St. ST6	24 B6		Sefton Rd. ST3	49 H
Rochford Way. ST3	43 G2		Russett Clo. ST3	56 C3		St Peters Clo. ST5	41 F5		Sefton St. ST1	31 E
Rock House Dri. ST12	59 F5		Rustington Av. ST3	49 H4		St Peters Walk. ST6	31 E2		Selbourne Dri. ST6	16 C
Rockfield Av. ST2	27 G4		Ruston Av. ST6	17 F5		St Thomas Pl. ST4	40 D6		Selby Clo. ST5	45 E
Roe La. ST5	45 E3		Rutherford Av. ST5	45 F5		St Vincent Pl. ST5	38 D2		Selby St. ST3	50 D
Roebuck St. ST4	41 G5		Rutherford Pl. ST4	40 B5		Salcombe Pl. ST1	31 H1		Selwood Clo. ST3	55 G
Rogate Clo. ST4	49 E1		Ruthin Rd. ST2	43 F1		Salem St. ST1	40 D1		Selworthy Rd. ST6	18 C
Rogers Av. ST5	28 D6		Rutland Pl. ST3	49 E3		Salisbury Av. ST1	41 F2		Selwyn St. ST4	47 F
Rogerstone Av. ST4	40 B6		Rutland St. ST1	31 E4		Salisbury St. ST6	24 B1		Settle Gro. ST3	56 C
Rolfe Clo. ST4	46 D6		Ruxley Ct. ST2	32 C6		Salkeld Pl. ST6	17 F6		Seven Arches Way. ST4	41 G
Roma Clo. ST3	55 G2		Ruxley Rd. ST2	32 C6		Salop Pl. ST3	45 H3		Sevenoaks Dri. ST3	56 D
Roman Dri. ST5	28 B3		Rycroft St. ST6	26 A2		Saltdean Clo. ST3	49 H6		Severn Dri. ST5	45 F
Romer Side. ST2	43 F4		Rydal Way. ST5	45 F3		Salters Clo. ST9	34 D5		Severn St. ST1	31 E
Romford Pl. ST3	56 D4		Ryder Rd. ST3	56 B2		Salters La. ST9	34 D5		Seymour St. ST1	32 A
Romney Av. ST5	28 C3		Rye Bank. ST5	39 G3		Samuel St. ST7	16 A1		*Shackleton Dri,	
Romney Gro. ST3	55 F2		Rye Bank Cres. ST5	39 G3		Sampson St. ST1	6 A2		Spitfire Way. ST6	23 H
Romsey Clo. ST2	43 G3		Ryebrook Gro. ST6	16 C4		Sandbach Rd. ST6	25 F6		Shackson Clo. ST1	41 F
Ronald St. ST3	49 F6		Ryecroft. ST5	39 F3		Sandcrest Pl. ST3	56 A2		Shaftesbury Av. ST6	25 E
Ronaldsway Dri. ST5	39 F1		Ryeland Clo. ST5	55 F2		Sandcrest Walk. ST3	56 A2		Shakespeare Clo. ST7	26 C
Ronson Av. ST4	46 B3		Rylestone Clo. ST3	56 D4		Sandford St, Crackley. ST5	22 C6		Shaldon Av. ST9	27 F
Rookery Av. ST3	48 C6		Sackville St. ST4	40 B2		Sandford St,			Shallowford Ct. ST1	41 E
Rookery La. ST4	46 C4		Saffron Clo. ST3	56 C5		Sandford Hill. ST3	49 F2		Shardlow Clo. ST4	42 D
Rope St. ST4	40 A3		Sage Clo. ST1	41 G1		Sandgate St. ST3	49 G5		Sharman Clo. ST4	40 C
Rose St. ST1	32 A4		St Aidens St. ST4	24 A1		Sandhurst Av. ST3	56 A1		Shaw St, Hanley. ST1	31 E
Roseacre. ST5	39 E5		St Andrews Cres. ST1	31 H1		Sandhurst Clo. ST5	29 G4		Shaw St,	
Roseacre Gro. ST3	56 A5		St Andrews Dri. ST5	38 D4		Sandhurst Pl. ST3	56 A2		Newcastle. ST5	39 F
Roseacre La. ST11	60 D3		St Andrews Sq. ST4	41 E5		Sandiway Pl. ST1	32 B2		Shawport Av. ST5	23 E
Rosebery St. ST6	16 C5		St Ann St. ST1	31 H5		Sandon Av. ST3	45 F2		Sheaf Pass. ST3	49 F
Rosehill Clo. ST2	27 E5		*St Ann Walk,			Sandon Old Rd. ST3	56 B4		Sheaf St. ST1	41 F
Roseland Cres. ST2	27 E5		St Ann St. ST1	31 H5		Sandon Rd. ST3	56 B3		Shearer St. ST1	6 A
Rosemary Pl. ST1	32 A1		St Annes Vale. ST6	18 D1		Sandon St. ST1	31 E6		Sheepwash. ST11	51 H
Rosendale Av. ST5	29 E2		St Anthonys Dri. ST5	39 E6		Sandown Pl. ST2	27 E3		Shefford Rd. ST5	44 D
Roseneath Pl. ST2	27 E5		St Bartholomews Clo.			Sandra Clo. ST6	24 D3		Shelburne St. ST4	46 D
Rosetree Av. ST4	46 B5		ST6	26 B1		Sandringham Cres. ST4	52 D1		Sheldon Gro. ST6	29 E
Rosevale Ct. ST5	22 C6					Sandwell Pl. ST3	55 H2		Sheldon St. ST6	31 E
Rosevale Rd. ST5	22 D6					Sandwick Cres. ST1	32 C3		Sheldrake Gro. ST4	49 E
Rosevale St. ST2	27 E5					Sandwood Cres. ST3	49 F2		Shelley Rd. ST2	27 E

Street	Ref
Tasmin Sq. ST1	32 A4
Tatton St. ST3	49 F6
Taunton Pl. ST5	28 D1
Taunton Way. ST2	43 G2
Taurus Gro. ST6	16 C4
Tavistock Cres. ST5	45 E2
Tavistock Pl. ST4	40 B3
Tawney Cres. ST3	50 D5
Tay Clo. ST3	49 E2
Taylor Av. ST5	29 H5
Taylor Rd. ST2	32 D2
Taylor St. ST5	29 H5
Taynton Clo. ST6	17 E2
Teal View. ST6	25 G3
Telford Way. ST6	16 D6
Tellwright Gro. ST5	29 F2
Tellwright St. ST6	25 E4
Templar Cres. ST5	29 G2
Templar Ter. ST5	29 G2
Temple St. ST4	47 H1
Templeton Av. ST2	43 G4
Tenbury Grn. ST2	43 F2
Tenby Gro. ST5	28 D1
Tennant Pl. ST5	29 G1
Tennyson Gdns. ST3	48 B6
Tercil Gro. ST3	56 C4
Terrington Dri. ST5	45 F5
Terry Clo. ST3	50 D4
Terson Way. ST3	50 B3
Tewkesbury Gro. ST2	32 D5
Tewson Grn. ST6	31 G1
Thackeray Dri. ST3	48 C6
Thames Rd. ST5	45 F4
Thanet Gro. ST3	48 D4
Thatchers Grn. ST3	54 B4
The Acres. ST5	38 A3
The Avenue, Basford. ST5	40 A1
The Avenue, Endon. ST9	20 B2
The Avenue, Forsbrook. ST11	60 E3
The Avenue, Hartshill. ST4	40 A5
The Beeches. ST5	29 H2
The Boulevard. ST6	24 B2
The Brackens. ST5	45 G6
The Brambles. ST5	45 G5
The Briars. ST5	39 G1
The Bridle Path. ST5	44 D4
The Brighton. ST5	37 G2
The Canal Mews. ST4	53 F4
The Close, Endon. ST9	20 B2
The Close, Weston Coyney. ST3	50 D2
The Coppice. ST6	31 G1
The Covert. ST5	45 H6
The Crescent, Newcastle. ST5	39 F6
The Crescent, Silverdale. ST5	37 G2
The Crescent, Trent Vale. ST4	46 C3
The Crescent, Weston Coyney. ST3	50 D3
The Croft. ST4	46 C2
The Crossway. ST5	29 H6
The Dams. ST11	51 G5
The Dell. ST5	37 H3
The Dingle. ST6	19 E3
The Dreys. ST4	53 E4
The Elms. ST5	29 H2
The Fieldway. ST4	52 B4
The Gables. ST5	29 H1
The Glade. ST5	45 F5
The Grange. ST3	50 C6
The Green, Baddeley Green. ST2	27 E1
The Green, Barlaston. ST12	59 G5
The Green, Brown Edge. ST6	19 E3
The Green, Caverswall. ST11	51 F4
The Green, Clayton. ST5	45 H5
The Greenway, May Bank. ST5	29 H6
The Greenway, Weston Coyney. ST4	52 B3
The Grove, Blythe Bridge. ST11	57 H5
The Grove, Newcastle. ST5	39 G6
The Grove, Smallthorne. ST6	25 F3
The Hollies. ST5	39 H2
The Hollow. ST11	51 G5
The Homestead. ST2	27 E2
The Lea. ST4	53 E4
The Limes. ST5	29 H1
The Mead. ST4	53 E4
The Meadows. ST9	20 C2
The Mews. ST5	30 A5
The Midway. ST5	39 F4
The Moat. ST3	50 C3
The Mount. ST5	28 C2
The Orchard. ST6	18 D2
The Orchards. ST3	48 A4
The Oval, Blurton. ST3	48 D6
The Oval, Werrington. ST9	35 G4
The Parade. ST5	37 H2
The Parks. ST4	53 H3
The Parkway, Hanley. ST1	41 G2
The Parkway, Newcastle. ST5	39 F6
The Parkway, Trentham. ST4	52 B3
The Pippins. ST5	45 G5
The Plaisaunce. ST5	45 F1
The Priory. ST9	20 C1
The Quadrangle. ST9	20 C3
The Quadrant. ST1	6 C2
The Roche. ST4	46 C2
The Rookery. ST5	37 H2
The Saplings. ST5	45 G5
The Spinney. ST5	45 H6
The Square, Meir. ST3	50 D6
The Square, Westlands. ST5	45 F1
The Squirrels. ST5	45 G5
The Strand. ST2	49 E4
The Thistles. ST5	38 D6
The Tudors. ST6	16 C6
The Village. ST5	37 E5
The Villas. ST4	46 D1
The Wood. ST3	50 D6
Thelma Av. ST6	19 E3
Theodore Rd. ST2	33 E6
Theresa Clo. ST4	46 D6
Third Av. ST2	33 H5
Thirlmere Gro. ST3	49 H5
Thirlmere Pl. ST5	45 G2
Thirsk Pl. ST5	37 F2
Thistleberry Av. ST5	38 D5
Thistleberry Parkway. ST5	38 D5
Thistleberry Villas. ST5	39 E5
Thistley Hough. ST4	46 C1
Thomas Av. ST5	29 E5
Thomas St. ST7	16 A1
Thompstone Av. ST5	28 D6
Thornburrow Dri. ST4	40 B5
Thorncliff Gro. ST1	32 B4
Thorndyke St. ST1	41 E2
Thorne Pl. ST3	50 D5
Thornham Clo. ST5	45 G6
Thornhill Rd. ST2	43 H4
Thornley Rd. ST6	24 D2
Thornton Rd. ST4	41 F4
Thornycroft Av. ST6	25 F4
Thorpe Grn. ST3	54 B3
Thorpe Way. ST2	43 H3
Three Mile La. ST5	37 E6
Thurlwood Dri. ST6	26 B4
Thursfield Pl. ST6	17 H6
Thursfield Walk. ST6	17 H6
Thurston Way. ST2	43 F4
Thyme Gro. ST3	56 C5
Tiber Dri. ST5	28 B3
Tidebrook Pl. ST6	16 C3
Tideswell Rd. ST3	49 F2
Tierney St. ST1	31 H4
Tilbrook Clo. ST2	43 F4
Tilehurst Pl. ST3	48 B6
Tilery La. ST3	53 H2
Tilery La. ST3	54 C1
Tillet Grn. ST3	50 D5
Tilson Av. ST4	40 D6
Timble Clo. ST2	43 F4
Times Sq. ST3	49 E4
Timmis St. ST1	41 E1
Timor Gro. ST4	53 F3
Timothy Clo. ST3	43 F6
Tintagel Pl. ST2	43 G4
Tintern Pl. ST5	28 D1
Tipping Av. ST3	56 D1
Tirley St. ST4	48 A2
Tissington Pl. ST3	57 E3
Tittensor Rd, Clayton. ST5	45 H2
Tittensor Rd, Tittensor. ST12	58 C5
Titterton St. ST4	47 G1
Tiverton Rd. ST2	43 F3
Toft End Rd. ST5	23 F5
Tolkien Way. ST4	40 D4
Toll Bar Rd. ST9	35 G4
Tomlinson St. ST6	24 A6
Tonbridge Av. ST6	25 F1
Toney Pl. ST2	42 C1
Tongue La. ST5	18 A2
Tontine St. ST1	6 C3
Tony Waddington Pl. ST4	42 C1
Topham Pl. ST2	42 C1
Tor St. ST1	31 H1
Torres Valley. ST1	32 A4
Torridan Clo. ST4	53 G5
Tower Sq. ST6	24 A2
Town Rd. ST1	6 C2
Townsend Pl. ST2	32 D6
Trade St. ST4	41 E5
Trafalgar Rd. ST4	40 B4
Trafalgar St. ST1	6 B1
Transport La. ST3	49 E4
Tranter Rd. ST2	33 E3
*Travers Ct, Temple St. ST5	47 H1
Travers St. ST6	30 B1
Trecastle Gro. ST3	56 A1
Tregaron Ct. ST2	34 B5
Tregenna Clo. ST3	56 C4
Tregew Pl. ST5	38 B2
Tregowan Clo. ST6	25 E2
Trent Gro. ST5	45 F4
Trent Rd. ST11	60 D2
Trent St. ST2	32 C6
Trent Ter. ST6	18 C6
Trent Valley Rd. ST4	46 C2
Trent Walk. ST1	41 H2
Trentfields Rd. ST2	26 D3
Trentham Ct. ST4	52 C4
Trentham Gdns Clo. ST4	52 C4
Trentham Gro. ST5	29 H5
Trentham Rd, Hem Heath. ST4	54 A4
Trentham Rd, Longton. ST3	49 E6
Trentham Rd, Westbury Park. ST5	44 A6
Trentley Rd. ST4	52 D3
Trentmill Rd. ST1	42 A1
Trentside Rd. ST6	18 C5
Trenton Clo. ST2	42 C1
Trevithick Clo. ST2	43 G5
Trevor Dri. ST11	51 F5
Trimley Way. ST2	43 E2
Tring Clo. ST2	43 F4
Triner Pl. ST6	26 A1
Trinity Ct. ST5	28 C1
Trinity Pl. ST2	33 E5
Trinity St. ST1	6 A3
Triton Walk. ST6	25 H4
Troutdale Clo. ST4	43 E6
Trowbridge Cres. ST3	43 F1
Trubshawe St. ST6	24 A6
Truro Pl. ST2	43 E1
Tudor Clo. ST4	46 D1
Tudor Ct. ST11	29 G3
Tudor Gro. ST5	29 G5
Tulip Gro. ST5	39 G2
Tulley Pl. ST2	32 D6
Tulsa Ct. ST2	42 C3
Tunbridge Dri. ST5	37 E2
Tunnicliffe Clo. ST3	49 H5
Turin Dri. ST5	38 C6
Turnberry Dri. ST4	52 D2
Turner Cres. ST5	28 C3
Turner St. ST1	31 H4
Turnhill Gro. ST5	29 F2
Turnhurst Rd. ST6	16 C2
Turnock St. ST2	33 F5
Tuscan St. ST3	49 F
Tuscan Way. ST5	28 E
Tutbury Gro. ST3	49 G
Tweed Gro. ST5	45 F
Tweed St. ST4	48 A
Twemlow St. ST1	31 E
Twigg St. ST2	32
Twyning Grn. ST3	54 B
Tyler Gro. ST6	24 C
Tyndall Pl. ST4	40 B
Tyne Way. ST5	45 F
Tyneham Gro. ST2	26 D
Tynwald Grange. ST5	39 E
Tyrell Gro. ST1	26 B
Tyson Grn. ST2	43 G
Ubberley Grn. ST2	43 F
Ubberley Rd. ST2	43 F
Uffington Par. ST2	43 F
Ufton Clo. ST3	54 B
Ullswater Av. ST6	24 B
Ulster Ter. ST4	46 D
Ulverston Rd. ST3	54 B
Umberleigh Rd. ST3	54 B
Underwood Rd. ST5	37 E
Unicorn Pl. ST6	16 C
Union Ct. ST1	6 B
Union St. ST1	6 B
Unity Av. ST1	31 H
Unwin St. ST6	25 F
Uplands Av, Great Chell. ST6	16 D
Uplands Av, Werrington. ST9	34 C
Uplands Croft. ST9	34 C
Uplands Dri. ST9	34 C
Uplands Rd. ST2	33 E
Upper Belgrave Rd. ST3	55 G
Upper Cres. ST4	40 B
Upper Cross St. ST3	49 F
Upper Furlong St. ST4	47 H
Upper Hillchurch St. ST1	6 D
Upper Huntbach St. ST1	6 D
Upper Market Sq. ST1	6 C
Upper Marsh. ST5	30 A
Upper Normacot Rd. ST3	49 G
Urmston Pl. ST3	54 B
Utterby Side. ST2	43 F
Uttoxeter Rd, Longton. ST3	49 F
Uttoxeter Rd, Meir. ST3	56 B
Vale Pl. ST1	6 A
Vale Pleasant. ST5	37 H
Vale St, Crackley. ST5	22 C
Vale St, Silverdale. ST5	37 G
Vale St, Stoke. ST4	41 E
Vale View. ST5	30 A
Valerian Way. ST3	56 C
Valley Park Way. ST3	48 B
Valley Rd. ST3	50 D
Venice Ct. ST5	38 C
Venn Pl. ST1	6 A
Ventnor Gro. ST3	54 B
Venton Clo. ST6	26 B
*Venture Way, Bradley Village. ST6	25 F
Verney Way. ST3	54 B
Vernham Side. ST2	43 F
Vernon Rd. ST4	41 F
Verona Gro. ST3	49 H
Vessey Ter. ST5	39 F
Vicarage Cres, Caverswall. ST11	51 F
Vicarage Cres, Newcastle. ST5	39 H
Vicarage Cres, Tittensor. ST12	58 C
Vicarage La, Barlaston. ST12	59 G
Vicarage La, Trent Vale. ST4	46 B
Vicarage Rd. ST4	40 C
Vichy Clo. ST5	38 C
Vickers Rd. ST6	17 E
Victoria Av. ST1	41 F
Victoria Clo. ST5	38 A
Victoria Park Rd. ST6	24 B
Victoria Pl. ST5	48 A
Victoria Rd, Newcastle. ST5	39 H

ctoria Rd,			
Stoke. ST4	41 H3		
ctoria Sq. ST1	6 A6		
ctoria St,			
Basford. ST4	40 A2		
ctoria St,			
Chesterton. ST5	28 C1		
ctoria St,			
Newcastle. ST5	39 H5		
ctoria St,			
Silverdale. ST5	38 A2		
enna Pl. ST5	38 D6		
enna Way. ST3	49 H3		
ggars Pl. ST5	38 D1		
lla St. ST4	47 E2		
lliers St. ST3	55 E1		
ncent St. ST1	32 A4		
ne Row. ST4	47 E1		
nebank St. ST4	47 E1		
scount Walk. ST3	56 B3		
vian Rd. ST4	48 B1		
owchurch Way. ST2	43 F3		
ade Av. ST5	30 A3		
ade St. ST6	25 F4		
adebridge Rd. ST2	43 E3		
adham St. ST4	40 D5		
ain Av, Cornhill. ST6	18 A5		
ain Av,			
Newcastle. ST5	38 D4		
ain Dri. ST4	46 B1		
ain St. ST6	24 D4		
ainwood Rise. ST4	46 C2		
akefield Rd. ST4	46 C3		
alcot Gro. ST2	42 C2		
alker Rd. ST6	16 D6		
alker St. ST6	24 B3		
alkersgreen Rd. ST5	22 B3		
alklate Av. ST5	40 A1		
allesley St. ST1	41 F2		
alley Pl. ST6	31 E1		
alley St. ST6	31 E1		
alleys Dri. ST5	40 A1		
allis Pl. ST2	33 E4		
allis St. ST4	48 B1		
allis Way. ST2	26 D4		
almer Pl. ST3	49 E2		
alney Gro. ST1	31 G3		
alnut Av. ST4	46 B5		
alnut Gro. ST5	22 B6		
alpole St. ST3	49 G2		
alsingham Gdns. ST5	45 G6		
alton Cres. ST4	47 G1		
alton Pl. ST5	28 D3		
alton Rd. ST4	46 C5		
Warburton Ct,			
Warburton St. ST6	31 E1		
arburton St. ST6	31 E1		
ard Pl. ST6	17 F6		
ardle La. ST2	27 F5		
ardle St. ST6	24 B2		
arminster Pl. ST3	48 D4		
armson Clo. ST3	43 F6		
arner St. ST1	6 B5		
arren Pl. ST3	49 G5		
arren Rd. ST6	17 F4		
arren St. ST3	49 F5		
arrington Rd. ST1	41 H3		
arrington St. ST4	48 B1		
arrlowheath Rd. ST5	22 A4		
arsill Gro. ST3	49 G3		
arwick Av, Clayton. ST5	45 H3		
arwick Av, Meir. ST3	56 B1		
arwick Gro. ST5	30 B6		
arwick St,			
Broad Meadow. ST5	28 C2		
arwick St,			
Hanley. ST1	41 E1		
asherwall La. ST9	34 C3		
asherwall St. ST2	43 G4		
ashington St. ST6	24 B3		
atchfield Clo. ST3	56 B1		
ater St, Boothen. ST4	47 E2		
ater St,			
Newcastle. ST5	39 H3		
ater St,			
Red Street. ST5	22 B3		
aterbeck Gro. ST4	53 G6		
aterdale Gro. ST3	49 H4		
atergate St. ST6	24 A2		
aterhead Rd. ST3	56 B2		
Waterloo Rd,			
Burslem. ST6	24 D6		
Waterloo Rd,			
Hanley. ST1	6 A1		
Waterloo St. ST1	31 H6		
Waters Edge. ST1	31 H2		
Waterside Dri. ST3	54 B4		
Watery La. ST3	55 H1		
Watford St. ST4	41 G4		
Watkin St. ST4	47 H1		
Watlands Av. ST5	29 G3		
Watlands View. ST5	29 G3		
Watson Rd. ST4	46 C4		
Watson St. ST4	40 D5		
Waveney Ct. ST5	45 G4		
Waveney Gro. ST5	45 G4		
Waveney Walk Nth. ST6	24 D1		
Waveney Walk Sth. ST6	24 D1		
Waverley Pl. ST5	45 F3		
Waverton Rd. ST2	43 H5		
Wayfield Gro. ST4	40 A4		
Wayside Av. ST5	29 H5		
Wayte St. ST1	31 F3		
Weaver Pl. ST5	45 G4		
Weaver St. ST1	6 B3		
Webb St. ST3	50 D5		
Webberley La. ST3	49 F5		
Webster Av. ST3	50 A2		
Webster St. ST5	39 H5		
Wedgwood Av. ST5	39 E6		
Wedgwood Dri. ST12	59 E3		
Wedgwood La. ST12	59 G2		
Wedgwood Pl. ST6	24 D5		
Wedgwood Rd. ST4	48 B1		
Wedgwood St,			
Burslem. ST6	24 D5		
Wedgwood St,			
Red Street. ST5	22 B2		
Wedgwood St,			
Wolstanton. ST5	30 A4		
Weighton Gro. ST2	43 H3		
Welbeck Pl. ST2	33 E4		
Welby St. ST4	47 H1		
Welch St. ST4	41 F6		
Weldon Av. ST3	50 D3		
Well St,			
Forsbrook. ST11	60 E2		
Well St,			
Hanley. ST1	6 D4		
Well St,			
Newcastle. ST5	39 G4		
Welland Gro. ST5	45 F4		
Wellbury Clo. ST4	59 E1		
Weller St. ST4	40 C4		
Wellfield Rd. ST4	43 E2		
Wellington Ct. ST1	31 H5		
Wellington Rd. ST1	31 H5		
Wellington St,			
Dimsdale. ST5	29 H4		
Wellington St,			
Hanley. ST1	31 H6		
Wellington Ter. ST1	31 H6		
Welsh Clo. ST3	55 G2		
Wem Gro. ST5	22 C3		
Wendling Clo. ST2	43 G3		
Wendover Gro. ST2	43 E3		
Wendy Clo. ST2	43 E3		
Wenger Cres. ST4	52 D4		
Wenham Dri. ST3	56 D4		
Wenlock Clo, Oxford. ST6	17 E2		
Wenlock Clo,			
Red Street. ST5	22 C3		
Wensleydale Clo. ST4	31 G1		
Wentworth Gro. ST1	26 B6		
Werburgh Dri. ST4	52 D4		
Werrington Rd. ST2	32 C6		
Wesker Pl. ST3	50 B3		
Wesley Pl. ST3	39 E4		
Wesley St,			
Blythe Bridge. ST11	60 D3		
Wesley St, Tunstall. ST6	24 B2		
Wessex Dri. ST4	53 E2		
West Av, Basford. ST5	40 A2		
West Av, Stoke. ST4	40 D5		
West Bank. ST4	40 D6		
West Brampton. ST5	39 G3		
West Cres. ST3	26 A6		
West Par. ST4	47 G2		
West St, Newcastle. ST5	39 H4		
West St, Porthill. ST5	30 A2		
West St, Silverdale. ST5	37 G2		
West St,			
Weston Coyney. ST3	50 D2		
West Ter. ST6	17 E4		
West View, Dimsdale. ST5	29 G4		
West View,			
Meir Heath. ST3	55 F5		
Westacre. ST1	32 C6		
Westbourne Dri. ST6	16 B5		
Westbury Clo. ST1	32 B3		
Westbury Rd. ST5	45 F5		
Westcliffe Av. ST3	45 F5		
Westerby Dri. ST9	34 C5		
Westerham Clo. ST4	52 C4		
Westfield Rd. ST2	33 E6		
Westhead Walk. ST1	41 E1		
Westland St. ST4	40 D5		
Westlands Av. ST5	39 E5		
Westmarsh Gro. ST6	25 E1		
Westmill St. ST1	41 H2		
Westminster Pl. ST4	52 D1		
Westmorland Clo. ST6	16 D2		
Weston Clo,			
Cross Heath. ST5	28 D6		
Weston Clo,			
Ash Bank. ST2	34 B4		
Weston Coyney Rd. ST3	49 G5		
Weston Ct. ST3	50 C4		
Weston Dri. ST3	50 C3		
Weston Rd. ST3	50 C4		
Weston St. ST3	49 G1		
Westonfields Dri. ST3	50 A5		
Westonview Av. ST3	49 G2		
Westport Lake Rd. ST6	24 A5		
Westport Rd. ST6	24 B4		
Westsprink Cres. ST3	49 H5		
Westwood Ct. ST1	31 H5		
Westwood Rd,			
Meir. ST3	50 C6		
Westwood Rd,			
Wolstanton. ST5	30 A3		
Wetherby Clo. ST5	28 C1		
Wetherby Rd. ST4	53 E3		
Wetley Av. ST9	35 H4		
Weybourne Av. ST2	27 E2		
Whalley Av. ST4	40 C6		
Wharf Pl. ST4	41 F5		
Wharf St. ST5	39 H3		
Wharfedale Walk. ST3	48 D5		
Whatmore St. ST6	25 G5		
Wheatfields. ST6	25 F1		
Wheatly Av. ST4	46 B1		
Whieldon Cres. ST4	47 G2		
Whieldon Rd. ST4	47 G1		
Whimpleside. ST2	43 E3		
Whitaker Rd. ST3	48 B4		
Whitchurch Gro. ST5	22 C4		
Whitcliffe Pl. ST3	48 B4		
Whitcombe Rd. ST3	50 C5		
Whitebeam Clo. ST5	22 B5		
Whitehaven Dri. ST1	31 F4		
Whitehead Rd. ST6	17 E5		
Whitehouse Rd,			
Abbey Hulton. ST2	32 D3		
Whitehouse Rd,			
Cross Heath. ST5	29 F6		
Whitesands Gro. ST3	56 C4		
Whitestone Rd. ST3	56 D5		
Whitethorn Av. ST12	59 E5		
Whitethorn Way. ST5	22 C5		
Whitfield Av. ST5	39 E5		
Whitfield Rd. ST6	18 A5		
Whitley Rd. ST6	17 H4		
Whitmore Av. ST4	34 D4		
Whitmore Rd,			
Butterton. ST5	44 B4		
Whitmore Rd,			
Trentham. ST4	52 A2		
Whitmore Rd,			
Westbury Park. ST5	44 A6		
Whitmore St. ST1	41 E1		
Whitridge Gro. ST2	43 H5		
Whittle Rd. ST3	56 D2		
Whygate Gro. ST1	32 C3		
Widecombe Rd. ST1	32 C2		
Wigmore Pl. ST3	49 F1		
Wilding Rd. ST6	18 A4		
Wileman Pl. ST4	48 B1		
Wileman St. ST4	48 B1		
Wilfred St. ST4	40 C4		
Wilkinson St. ST6	24 B3		
Wilks St. ST6	24 B1		
Willatt Pl. ST2	26 C4		
Willdale Gro. ST1	32 C4		
Willeton St. ST2	42 D1		
Willfield La. ST6	19 E3		
William Av. ST3	57 E2		
William Birch Ct. ST2	42 D3		
William Birch Rd. ST2	42 D3		
William Clo. ST11	60 F2		
William Clowes St. ST6	24 C6		
William Fiske Ct. ST4	46 C3		
William Rushton Rd.			
ST6	25 G4		
William St. ST4	42 A6		
William Ter. ST6	17 E4		
Williamson Av. ST6	18 A4		
Williamson St. ST6	24 B3		
Willotts Hills Clo. ST5	22 B4		
Willow Clo. ST5	22 B5		
Willow Gro. ST3	48 A5		
Willow Row. ST3	49 E5		
Willow Way. ST11	60 E1		
Willowcroft Rise. ST11	57 E3		
Willowdale Av. ST4	47 G2		
Willowfield Dri. ST4	53 G4		
Willows Dri. ST3	55 G5		
Willowood Grn. ST3	57 E2		
Wilmot Clo. ST5	29 E6		
Wilmot Dri. ST6	28 D6		
Wilmot Gro. ST3	49 F1		
Wilson Rd. ST4	46 D6		
Wilson St,			
Newcastle. ST5	39 G2		
Wilson St,			
Stanfield. ST6	25 E4		
Wilton Av. ST9	35 H4		
Wilton St. ST5	39 F1		
Wiltshire Gro. ST5	45 H3		
Wimberry Dri. ST5	22 B4		
Wimborne Av. ST3	54 B4		
Winchester Av. ST2	43 F1		
Winchester Dri. ST5	44 D3		
Windermere Rd. ST5	45 G3		
Windermere St. ST1	31 E4		
Windmill Clo. ST3	55 F5		
Windmill Hill. ST3	55 E6		
Windmill St. ST1	6 D2		
Windmill View. ST9	35 E4		
Windrush Clo. ST4	53 F6		
Windsmoor St. ST4	47 F1		
Windsor Av. ST3	49 G6		
Windsor Rd. ST4	46 D6		
Wingate Walk. ST4	54 C4		
Winghay Clo. ST6	23 H6		
Winghay Pl. ST6	17 F6		
Winghouse La. ST12	58 A6		
Wingrove Av. ST3	55 G1		
Winifred Gdns. ST3	54 B2		
Winifred St. ST1	31 F4		
Winnipeg Clo. ST4	53 F2		
Winpenny Rd. ST5	23 E5		
Winsford Av. ST3	50 A5		
Winslow Grn. ST2	43 F2		
Winston Pl. ST2	32 D6		
Winston Ter. ST6	29 G3		
Winterbourne Gro. ST3	49 H4		
Winterside Clo. ST5	22 B4		
Winton Field St. ST4	41 G5		
Winton Sq. ST4	41 F4		
Wise St. ST3	55 F1		
Witchford Cres. ST3	54 B4		
Withies Rd. ST4	46 B3		
Withington Rd. ST6	17 E4		
Withnell Grn. ST6	17 E3		
Withystakes Rd. ST9	35 F3		
Witney Walk. ST3	54 B4		
Woburn Clo. ST4	58 D1		
Wolfe St. ST4	41 E6		
Wolseley Rd,			
Dimsdale. ST5	29 G4		
Wolseley Rd,			
Oak Hill. ST4	46 D3		
Wolstanton Rd. ST5	28 D2		
Wolstern Rd. ST3	49 G1		
Wood Pl. ST3	50 D6		
Wood St. ST3	49 E3		
Wood Ter. ST1	41 F1		
Woodall St. ST1	31 F3		
Woodbank St. ST6	24 C6		
Woodberry Av. ST4	46 C2		
Woodberry Clo. ST4	46 C2		
Woodbridge Rd. ST5	45 G6		

Woodend St. ST4	48 C1	Woodside Pl. ST2	27 E5
Woodgate St. ST3	56 C1	Woodstock Clo. ST5	39 H1
Woodhall Pl. ST5	37 E1	Woodstone Av. ST9	20 A3
Woodhead Rd. ST2	32 D1	Woodvale Cres. ST9	20 B1
Woodhouse La. ST6	18 B4	Woodville Pl. ST3	50 C6
Woodhouse St. ST4	41 F6	Woodville Rd. ST3	50 C6
Woodingdean Clo. ST3	49 G2	Woodville Ter. ST3	50 D6
Woodkirk Clo. ST6	17 E2	Woodward St. ST1	31 H2
Woodland Av,		Woolliscroft Av. ST5	30 A6
Dimsdale. ST5	29 H3	Woolliscroft Rd. ST2	33 E6
Woodland Av, Norton in		Woolrich St. ST6	30 B1
the Moors. ST6	26 B1	Worcester Pl. ST2	43 G1
Woodland Gro. ST6	25 E3	Worth Clo. ST3	49 G3
Woodland St. ST6	24 B2	Worthing Pl. ST3	48 D4
Woodlands Gro. ST3	55 G6	Wren View. ST3	49 G6
Woodlands La. ST11	60 F3	Wrenbury Clo. ST5	22 B4
Woodlands Rd. ST4	46 B4	Wrenbury Cres. ST2	43 E3
Woodman St. ST2	26 D4	Wright Av. ST5	45 F5
Woodpark La. ST3	55 G3	Wrighton Clo. ST2	42 C2
Woodside Av. ST6	19 E4	Wroxham Way. ST5	45 F5
Woodside Cres. ST5	45 H5	Wulstan Dri. ST5	39 G1
Woodside Dri. ST3	55 G6	Wulstan Rd. ST6	30 D2

Wycliffe St. ST6	24 C6	Yew Tree Av. ST3	48 A
Wye Rd. ST5	45 F4	York Clo. ST11	60 N
Wymondley Gro. ST4	53 F5	York Pl. ST5	39 C
Wyndham Rd. ST3	54 B4	York Rd. ST3	50 D
Wynford Pl. ST2	43 E3	York St, Hanley. ST1	6 A
Wynstay Ct. ST5	44 B5	York St,	
		Newcastle. ST5	39 H
Yale St. ST6	24 B6	Youlgreave Av. ST2	42 D
Yardley St. ST6	18 C6	Youlton Pl. ST2	43 E
Yardley Walk. ST3	54 B5	Young St. ST6	16 C
Yarmouth Walk. ST3	30 B1	Younger St. ST4	41 H
Yarnbrook Gdns. ST6	25 H2	Yoxall Av. ST4	40 C
Yarnfield Clo. ST3	50 C6		
Yarrow Pl. ST3	56 C5	Zamenhof Gro. ST6	25 C
Yateley Clo. ST2	43 E2	Zennor Gro. ST2	43 E
Yates St. ST1	6 A6	Zetland Pl. ST3	54 C
Yaxley Ct. ST5	45 G6	Zetland Walk. ST3	54 C
Yaxley Pl. ST3	54 C4	Zion St. ST6	24 D
Yeaman St. ST4	47 E1	Zodiac Dri. ST6	16 C
Yeldham Pl. ST3	54 B5		
Yeovil Pl. ST3	54 B5		
Yew Pl. ST5	22 B5		